About the Author

John Woolmer works part time on the staff of Holy Trinity Leicester running a church plant; he also speaks for ReSource (Anglican Renewal Ministries). He preaches widely, leading missions and parish weekends, particularly on the themes of healing and prayer, and lectures regularly at two theological colleges.

John has led missions in Zambia, Kenya, Tanzania, Uganda, N Argentina and spoken at a Wycliffe Bible translators conference in Papua New Guinea.

His current writings are three books in the 'Thinking Clearly' series on Prayer, Healing and Deliverance, and Angels, all published by Monarch; and The Grand Surprise (Butterflies and the Kingdom of God), which reflects his main hobby.

He and his wife Jane have four grown up children who all serve the Lord in various ways.

To my Angel. Luv Kelly xx

Angels

OF GLORY & DARKNESS

JOHN WOOLMER

**MONARCH
BOOKS**

Oxford, UK & Grand Rapids, Michigan, USA

Some of the material in this book was previously published in "Thinking Clearly about Angels" by John Woolmer.

First published in the UK in 2006 by Monarch Books
(a publishing imprint of Lion Hudson plc),
Mayfield House, 256 Banbury Road, Oxford OX2 7DH.
Tel: +44 (0)1865 302750 Fax: +44 (0)1865 302757
Email: monarch@lionhudson.com
www.lionhudson.com

ISBN-13: 978-1-85424-736-0 (UK)
ISBN-10: 1-85424-736-0 (UK)
ISBN-13: 978-1-0-8254-6122-4 USA)
ISBN-10: 0-8254-6122-7 (USA)

Distributed by:
UK: Marston Book Services Ltd, PO Box 269,
Abingdon, Oxon OX14 4YN;
USA: Kregel Publications, PO Box 2607,
Grand Rapids, Michigan 49501

Unless otherwise stated, Scripture quotations are taken from the Holy Bible, New International Version, © 1973, 1978, 1984 by the International Bible Society. Used by permission of Hodder & Stoughton Ltd. All rights reserved.

The text paper used in this book has been made from wood independently certified as having come from sustainable forests.

British Library Cataloguing Data
A catalogue record for this book is available from the British Library.

Printed and bound in Great Britain by Cox & Wyman Ltd, Reading

Dedication

For Susie and Hugh, Katy and Ben in their
first years of marriage.

Acknowledgements

With grateful thanks for all those who have
shared their stories, especially new friends
from Papua New Guinea, and to Monarch
Books for their usual courtesy, gentle critique
and constant encouragement.

Contents

Introduction

TIME WAS WHEN ANGELS were the subjects of erudite theological discussions, magnificent medieval frescoes and occasional controversies. The angel guarding the northwest corner of the wagon roof in my former parish of Shepton Mallet is well peppered with grapeshot, fired in 1645 by Cromwell's soldiers in the English Civil War. Godly Puritans regarded the carved images of angels as highly offensive.

This book is written to defend the existence of angels, to look at their true role as messengers of God, and to warn that there are such beings as fallen angels. Not all spiritual experiences are helpful. Each encounter needs to be tested. The testimonies included in this book are mainly from people that I know personally and I would vouch for them as credible witnesses. As a mathematician, I look for the simplest solution to complicated problems. In many of the testimonies, in this and other books, it is simplest to accept them at face value and to believe that God did send an angel to guide, protect, comfort or to speak to people.

Angels are part of our heritage. Churches are full of angels in stained glass windows, or carved on magnificent roofs. Great painters have spent hours depicting them on famous canvasses and many bookshops allow plenty of space to an assortment of books on the subject. Nowadays, angels are either dismissed as part of a belief system that is no longer sustainable or welcomed, uncritically, as the gateway to an exciting spiritual world.

Angels are seen either as part of an ancient mythology

which is well past its sell-by date or as the road map to our spiritual future. Almost on demand, they can unlock the keys to true spiritual awareness and knowledge. I am unpersuaded by either viewpoint. I want to argue that angels are an ever-present reality, but unseen by most of us including myself.

Angels, quite simply, are God's messengers, who throughout eternity worship the living God. From time to time, they have earthly duties – probably far more than any of us are aware of. These involve protection, guidance and occasionally a lifting of the spiritual curtain to such an extent that both men and women are unexpectedly brought to a life-changing encounter with the living God.

The angels of glory give some people a glimpse of life 'beyond the veil' where tears, sorrow, illness, accident and even death are no more. They give us a foretaste of Paradise and a fleeting experience of what we can become when this life is ended.

Sadly, not all the angels were content with this role. A third of them seem to have rebelled. This rebellion has caused chaotic cosmic conflict and disastrous deception all around our planet. Angels of glory became angels of darkness. Angels of darkness are at their most dangerous when pretending to be angels of light. Deception has always been one of Satan's most effective weapons.

This short book tells a number of stories, which hopefully will point us back to the angels of the Bible. Hopefully, too, they will lead us away from seeking spirit guides and other psychic phenomena, which pretend to lead people to God and ensnare them in false spiritual self-fulfilment.

We live in an age, at least in our tired Western world, which desperately needs to rediscover spiritual reality. The angels of darkness are a warning to remind us how easily we are deceived – especially by offers of quick spiritual fixes. The angels of glory take us back to those critical moments when, for some of us, God's plans unfolded with an unforgettable and brilliant clarity.

If any of the recorded experiences in this book are true experiences of the angelic world, then they are pointers back to the *far more important truths* about the angels at Bethlehem and the angels beside the empty tomb on the first Easter Day.

If those two great stories are true, then there is hope for humanity. This hope transcends the horrors of war, suicide bombers with their false view of Paradise, tsunamis, earthquakes, AIDS, global warming and even death itself. This hope is summed up by some famous words 'The light shines in the darkness, but the darkness has not overcome it' (John 1:5, ASB).

CHAPTER 1

Two Demons and an Angel

'ISN'T IT TIME WE STOPPED conniving with all this medieval mumbo-jumbo?' An elderly clergyman was addressing the bishop. The bishop, who was chairing a conference which was taking place in his splendid medieval cathedral, smiled benignly. The conference, to which all the diocesan clergy had been summoned, was mainly about healing. But the more controversial area of deliverance (exorcism to some) had been mentioned, thereby dismaying those with more liberal theological views. The bishop turned to me as one of his panel of speakers. 'John, what do you have to say to that?' Encouraged by finding myself sitting next to a psychiatrist who also believed in the spiritual reality of this sort of problem, I replied unusually briefly:

'If you find yourself praying for a woman in a Zambian village where no one except the local priest speaks English (and he doesn't speak it very well) and a voice speaks through the woman and says in perfect Oxbridge English, *"Go away, I am not leaving this person!"* it is difficult to find a rational twenty-first-century interpretation. It is much simpler and wiser to believe that you are involved in a supernatural encounter like some of those recorded in the early chapters of Mark's Gospel.'

There was a stunned silence in the cathedral followed by a ripple of applause. Most people seemed relieved at my assertions that the Gospel accounts needn't be discarded, that the world we live in can't be rationalized and the supernatural dimension cannot be ignored.

Mutwe Wa Nkoko in May 1992

Mutwe Wa Nkoko is a small village, deep in the bush, in the Luapula Province in Northern Zambia. My wife Jane and I, together with our friend Martin Cavender[1] and his son Henry arrived late one Monday evening to a rapturous, typically Zambian welcome. We were accompanied by Archdeacon Tobias Kaoma and some other leading members of the Zambian Anglican Church. En route, we paid a courtesy call to the local chief. His household was in chaos, with sickness and worry concerning a daughter who was about to give birth. We prayed for them all and gave some small gifts of food. About a mile from the village we were met by hundreds of dancing, smiling people. They had garlands of flowers to give us and greeted us, dancing as they sang '*Sangale sangale* (let's be joyful)'. In the midst of a life-threatening drought, this was pretty impressive. We left our vehicle and joined in the fun. The village seemed quite small: a little church, a good deep well, a few houses and, in the distance, a school whose roof had been blown off in a storm some eighteen months earlier.

We washed in steaming hot water in a little stockade under the brilliant clear light of the Southern Cross and other stars of the bright African sky. There was a camp fire which involved food, singing, drama and much laughter. The main drama was about a man who tried to steal from his neighbour, but first he had to steal a bone from someone else to silence the neighbour's dog!

We went to bed happily and looking forward to two useful days of speaking, praying and discovering the extent and effect of the drought. The next morning, a crowd of about 500 gathered. We held a joyful service in the open air. After much singing and dancing, led by the exuberant members of the Mother's Union (clad in smart white turbans and blue *chitengas* – the brightly coloured full-length skirts worn by all the women), I preached about drawing water from the wells of salvation (Isaiah 12:3). It seemed appropriate in a village whose deep, cool well was sustaining them in a time of drought.

It was all very quiet and good-natured. Blue Charaxes butterflies danced from one great tree to another, providing me with a pleasant distraction. At the end of the morning, we invited people to join us for a time of prayer in the nearby church.

I was used to spiritual battles in Luapula, but nothing had prepared me for the ferocious battle that erupted. Tobias Kaoma, an experienced prayer and exorcist, was surrounded by a group of screaming women. The rest of us found that we only had to utter a word of prayer, or stretch out our hands towards someone, and they started to flutter their eyelids, shake violently, collapse to the ground, or even start slithering across the floor in a passable imitation of the local snake. Henry, the youngest member of the team, who had come as a late addition to the group to make a video, made an understandably swift exit.

In the midst of this maelstrom, Jane, my wife, called me over and said, 'Listen to this.' One of the women, or to be more accurate the spirit that was speaking through her, said, *'Go away, I am not leaving this person!'* She was speaking in perfect Oxbridge English – Zambians normally speak

English with a soft, lilting accent, but this woman's voice was harsh and powerful. We made little progress and retired for a simple lunch somewhat bruised and chastened. It was one of the few occasions that prayers of deliverance didn't seem to have much effect.

After a quick visit to a maize field, where I was shown the devastating effect of the drought on their crops, I returned to speak to the gathering crowd.

Speaking against the local demons

It was not my normal style, but I felt convinced that we had to stand against the local principalities and powers – especially Masonda, the black snake spirit, and Malenga, the water spirit. Both these names came up frequently when we asked people what was troubling them. The black snake was probably the emblem of local witchcraft. It seemed likely that many of the local mothers sought protection from the medicine men while also bringing their babies to the church for baptism.

Before speaking, I made a public prayer against these two demonic powers – *fallen angels* in biblical terms. I then challenged the congregation to stop hesitating between two opinions, to choose Christ and to throw away all charms, fetishes and potions from the local witch doctors. The response was laughter – not the friendly, good-natured laughter of the morning – but hollow, sinister, mocking laughter.

I asked Tobias, who was a wonderfully enthusiastic interpreter, what was happening. He said, 'They are saying – we have so little and now you are telling us to throw things away.' For a split second, I could sense their devastating logic. What right had I, a rich Westerner on only my second visit to Zambia, to challenge their culture and to tell them to throw away some of their most precious possessions?

The anger of God

Suddenly, I felt overwhelmed. For almost the only time in my life, I felt what I can only describe as the anger of God. The fact that I was an ignorant visiting Westerner didn't seem important – what mattered was that God was honoured and that meant that the demonic powers had to be opposed. People had to make a choice. No longer could they oscillate between two opinions. Even now, years later, I find it quite awesome to write about that afternoon. I spoke – I have no idea what – firm, even harsh words. I have never spoken like that before or since.

When I had finished, I felt shattered. I felt that I had failed, going way over the top. I don't remember much about the rest of the day. We had a session planned with Father James Chungolo, the local priest, and his healing team. I was so exhausted that I left Martin Cavender to speak to them; while Jane had a good session with the local Mother's Union, who are a tower of strength, both spiritually and socially, in rural Zambia.

After another hard night on a mattress on the floor with bats above, mosquitoes all around, spiders on the floor and the possibility of snakes outside, I felt distinctly unenthusiastic about the dawning of Wednesday morning. At least our prayer group back in Shepton Mallet would have been praying for us during the previous evening.

The angel around the church

The next morning we began with a communion service in the little church. About 300 people were crammed inside. I tried to ignore a substantial wasp busying itself with building a nest behind the altar, close to where we were sitting.

Eventually, it was time to preach. I could think of nothing to say. In desperation (or inspiration?), I asked Tobias Kaoma to give his testimony. Tobias was about sixty; his beloved wife Prisca had died, only a month earlier, at the age of forty-nine. Despite his very evident grief, Tobias had left his parish in Chipili to accompany us and to act as our leader and chief exorcist.

His eyes lit up as he testified to his conversion, his calling to the priesthood (when working as a head teacher) and about the day two years earlier when he had been spontaneously, and unexpectedly, deeply touched by the Holy Spirit. (I well remember that afternoon, a good friend of mine was speaking: I, I am ashamed to say was falling asleep – only to be awakened by the sight and sound of Tobias leaping around and praising God in many different languages. Tobias was transformed that afternoon, and a discerning friend of mine described him as the most powerful confronter of demons that he had ever met.)

His testimony was lifting everyone's spirits, but while he was still speaking, a tall dark lady glided out of the congregation. 'Could I say something?' she asked. For a woman, not even belonging to the Mother's Union, to interrupt a visiting leader was culturally unheard of, but Tobias, graciously and characteristically, gave way.

Her story was simple, its effect dramatic. As she spoke, her face shone with a lovely light. She spoke in Bemba, the local language. Early that morning, she and some friends had walked in the half-light from her village to the church. She, and one of her companions, had noticed a figure dressed in *white* following slowly along the path. While she peeled off into the bushes beside the church, the figure went round the other side. She then went around the church expecting to see the person. There was no one to be seen (the ground is quite open with a few trees and some *shambas* – Zambian huts).

As she spoke, her face glowed. The crowded congregation was deeply moved. Zambians do not wear *white* clothes. The Mother's Union welcomed her and symbolically placed one of their turbans on her head. Everyone felt that she had seen an angel – who had been sent to cleanse the church from the battles of the previous day. *It was, and remains, the most obviously supernatural experience of my life.*

The contrast with the futile battles of the previous day was remarkable; the whole atmosphere in the church was quite different. There was a sort of spiritual electricity in the air. It felt a little like the occasion in the Gospels where Luke writes 'the power of the Lord was present for him to heal the sick' (Luke 5:17). No one can conjure up these times; they are a sovereign gift from God!

I preached a simple evangelistic sermon. I asked those who would like to respond to stand up and come forward. Two young men stood up, and then the floodgates opened. We prayed for about forty; then for another sixty, including the local headman. During all this time of prayer, only one demon showed up. The man concerned was taken outside (always wisest to take people away from the limelight – demons are exhibitionists and seem to gain strength when lots of people are around) and evil powers were banished quickly and silently! Then we continued in prayer for the leaders and for many others to be healed, released from any evil oppression, and to be filled with the Holy Spirit.

Lunchtime came, the Blue Charaxes butterflies were courting around the tree nearest to the church, then it was time to leave. We left with much sadness, but also with great joy and a feeling of 'mission accomplished'.

We paid a return visit to the local chief. This time there was great joy. Two hours earlier, his granddaughter had been safely born, the mother was well, and other members of the household were better. We prayed and gave thanks for the little girl and retreated with an honoured gift – a live chicken which entertained us, during the long dusty car journey, by pecking at Martin's trousers.

Mutwe's reputation confirmed

Two years later, part of a team that I was leading revisited Mutwe. They found it tough going, but the lady who had seen the angel was a very visible part of the church and Father James was providing dynamic leadership.

In another part of Zambia, I was talking to a remarkable priest who at the age of eighty, in a mining town on the copper-belt, was still physically building new churches and evangelizing new areas. He said that Mutwe was the darkest place that he'd ever visited and that he'd had some terrible battles with demons there.

Clearly Mutwe is a place that has lived up its name (which literally means the village of the severed chicken's head!) and there is work still to be done there. But gradually as the Christian gospel takes a deeper root there, the powers of darkness will be driven back.

Spiritual outcomes from the angel's visit

There were a number of positive outcomes from this visit. James Chungolo was greatly inspired and twice came to help me minister in other parts of the Luapula Province. On one occasion, he cycled fifty kilometres with a flat tyre to help us.

He, too, had become a powerful exorcist and I saw him in action helping to deliver a young man who grunted, non-stop, like a pig! He also did battle, in the open air at Mwenda, with a spirit which he heard speaking in French through one of the local leaders. Most of all, his prayers deeply affected one of my team. Alison Morgan, in her brilliant book *The Wild Gospel*[2] writes:

In 1999, I had the opportunity to leave domestic responsibilities behind and to step briefly into the world of sub-Saharan Africa. I found myself flung into unexpected intimacy with a small team of almost complete strangers. *It was an experience which changed my life.* As I watched myself slowly take shape in their eyes, it was as if they were holding up a mirror, a mirror of affirmation and encouragement, a mirror which seemed to show me for the first time who I really was – strengths, weaknesses, idiosyncrasies and all. It was an astonishing experience, like going back to the beginning and starting again, and for the first time seeing the real me, the person God had created rather than the one pain had tried to form, and knowing myself to be totally and utterly acceptable, my blemishes covered by love.

At the end of our stay we were put in pairs during a service to pray for one another, and I found myself with

Father James Chungolo. I have no idea what he said, for he prayed in Bemba; but I could feel the Holy Spirit washing over me, prickling and pressing like a physical presence, and suddenly it seemed to me that I was like one of the half built houses we had seen so often as we travelled, made of baked earthen bricks but with no mortar between them. As he prayed I felt cement being poured over the walls, settling down between the bricks and drying in the warmth of the sun – and I understood that I was loved.

That experience helped to release Alison into a powerful new ministry which has taken her worldwide and into leadership in a number of key organisations. It is very doubtful, that without the visitation of the angel to Mutwe, that James Chungolo would have had the confidence to pray with Alison or to confront the powers of darkness with such faith.[3]

Spiritual outcomes – The Diocesan Registrar

Not long afterwards, Martin Cavender found himself in a difficult pastoral situation in England. After a long Sunday of ministry, the husband of a very committed local Christian asked for prayer. He was on the fringes of the church and had a violent temperament. He was an ex-guardsman, very large, and his wife showed signs of physical battering. Martin and two others engaged in a time of prayer, which became quite difficult, violent, and dangerous. Eventually the man was 'clothed and in his right mind', and a considerable healing process seemed to have begun. After Martin debriefed with other members of his prayer team, one lady, quite new to this sort of ministry, remarked innocently 'Didn't you see the four golden angels in each corner of the room as we were praying?' After the experiences in Zambia, Martin was rather less surprised than he would have been a few years earlier, when he had been confined to the relative safety of being the chief legal officer for the Diocese of Bath and Wells.

Spiritual outcomes – Hesitant Henry

Martin's son Henry came as a late addition to our team to Zambia. A priest dropped out at very short notice, and Martin suggested that his son Henry came, mainly to make a film of the trip. Henry, not yet a Christian, was both intrigued and scared by what he was required to film. It wasn't difficult to film his father giving radio and TV interviews even if it was surprising to see the church taken so seriously by the national media. It wasn't hard to shoot the exuberant Zambian worship, so refreshingly different from what he was used to at home. It was rather harder to watch people being prayed for – and apparently benefiting from the experience. It seemed both intrusive and frightening to film the people who seemed troubled by malevolent spirits. These people were mainly young women, often with babies on their backs.

When Henry returned to England, he spent his gap year living in Bath, and frequently found his friends asking him about things that he had seen in Africa. When he reported what he had seen and heard the usual reaction was 'You must be joking' followed by a turned back and a walking away. The strange thing was that the next day the same people used to come back and say, 'Tell me again what you saw in Africa.'

For eight years, Henry remained on a spiritual knife-edge – believing and yet not quite committed. He married, and he and his wife started attending an Assemblies of God church. But still he remained just beyond the fringe, convinced yet strangely unmoved.

Then one night, Henry dreamed that, with his wife, he was walking down a street in a Cornish seaside town. The main street had a large hotel in it, with a very clear sign outside which read 'Before going on the beach you need to register here'. The day was beautiful, so they ignored the notice, in common with everyone else. When they arrived on the beach it was brilliant clean sand, blue sky – and glorious sea. Then quite suddenly the sky turned black, the sea boiled up, the waves crashed, and bolts of fire began to rain down on the beach, which was now covered with screaming running people. As they raced for cover, trying to get back to the hotel to register, Henry felt a lump of brimstone hit his leg. All he knew was that he must get back to register at the hotel, which previously they had ignored. People were dying around them – and then Henry woke up.

He was baptized, by immersion, the very next Sunday. The dream had woken him up! His mother arrived for the service. She was a little late, having driven 200 miles. Henry was just about to be immersed, and was explaining to the congregation that he had seen it all in Zambia, but had delayed making a real profession of faith until now. In his testimony, he described himself as 'Hesitant Henry'.

Angelic experiences change people's faith

Meanwhile, I remain profoundly grateful to the Lord for releasing one angel whose visitation had such an effect in Mutwe which then produced spiritual ripples which touched so many completely different people! *There is an almost inevitable fruit from authentic angelic experiences –* many people's faith will be deepened and their confidence in God will grow.

I wish that my sceptical cathedral critic could have the chance to experience this! The church has enough problems battling with the powers of darkness without being hindered by leaders who deny the truth of part of the basic teaching of Jesus as recorded in all the Gospels. What is 'medieval mumbo-jumbo' to some people is a perfectly normal and natural experience to others.

I told a group of ninety-nine evangelists in Northern Tanzania about my cathedral encounter – their spontaneous reaction was to roar with laughter and to ask *'How can anyone be so stupid?!'* Telling the same story to African pastors, Bible translators in Papua New Guinea or church members in Argentina, I got the same reaction – except from a retired bishop. He asked, cautiously, 'Is there reality behind all this fear and superstition?' He seemed greatly relieved when I assured him that there is!

This short book is written to give some examples of the different ways in which people encounter angels, the dangers of spiritual deception and the reality of the spiritual opposition. It is written to show that we would be wise to be open to the ways and word of God even when they include demons and angels. *We cannot and must not spend our time seeking out these experiences.* We always need to test what is happening in the clear light of Scripture. Angels appear, and are experienced, in many different ways. It is to this matter we now turn.

Notes

1. In 1992, Martin Cavender left his safe job as Registrar of the Diocese of Bath and Wells to administer Springboard – the archbishop's initiative on evangelism. In 2004, he became director of ReSource, Anglican renewal ministries' new initiative.
2. Alison Morgan, *The Wild Gospel*, Oxford: Monarch, 2004, p. 303.
3. Both Tobias Kaoma and James Chungolo have now died. Their faithful ministries did much to build up the Anglican Church in what is now the new Diocese of Luapula in Northern Zambia.

CHAPTER 2

Angels – Are You Serious?

İN THIS CHAPTER, we hear from a number of reliable witnesses about their experiences with angels. We consider some of the different ways in which people see and experience angels and compare these with some well-known stories from the Bible. In all these experiences, angelic help came unsought. This is quite different from the records of many modern books and even some Christian websites which seem to imply that angels can be called up almost at will. The record of the Bible is crystal clear: angels appear at God's behest. Only Jesus, at the time of his arrest, said he could call up a legion of angels – and he chose not to do so!

When I was first writing about angels, my youngest daughter, then aged eighteen, asked, 'Daddy, what do angels look like?' It seemed a rather good question.

What do angels look like?

Angels appear, or are experienced, in a number of ways. Some people see what one might call 'traditional' angels (winged creatures, tall, bright, impressive and instinctively recognizable). Others receive unexpected assistance from someone who appears to be a human helper, who suddenly disappears and whose intervention doesn't fit any reasonable human explanation. This is perhaps the most common type of 'angelic' encounter. A third type of experience usually, but not always, in war-time, is when people are under attack and, inexplicably, the attackers withdraw or run away. Subsequent encounters with the attackers reveal that they were terrified by people, usually dressed in white, protecting those that they wanted to attack. A fourth type of experience is when people sense the presence of angels: hearing them singing, hearing their wings rustling, seeing an unusual light, occasionally even hearing an audible voice. We shall find, at the end of the chapter, that the Bible gives examples of all these types of experience.

Traditional angels

As illustrations, I have chosen four accounts. The first increased the impetus for prayer before the famous elections in South Africa which, peacefully, dismantled apartheid; the second sealed the conversion of a young man who was to become a leading writer and vicar of a large Anglican church; the third took place when an internationally renowned speaker was involved in a mission in England and the fourth was a gracious encounter which helped bring healing to a very distressed parent.

Other stories, in this and later chapters, will take us all over the world. The common thread is that the angels came as God's messengers to situations where God chose to intervene more directly than at other times.

An angel in South Africa
In the final decades of the twentieth century, the church faced huge pressure in many parts of the world. In South

Africa, the churches played a very important part in the dismantling of apartheid. Michael Cassidy tells the story in his powerful book *A Witness For Ever*[1].

Cassidy tells of a South African colonel deep in prayer on 23 March 1994, just a few weeks before the South African elections, which were to bring Nelson Mandela to power. The situation was very tense, many were praying, many despairing.

Colonel Johan Botha, a Christian, who after witnessing the appalling riots in Soweto in June 1976 had turned to God with even deeper intercession, was praying (unusually for him) in English.

He said, 'God, what is it that you want for us, and what do you want for South Africa?' Immediately, he saw an angel, bathed in a brilliant, indescribable light which hid his face. The angel said, 'I want South Africa on its knees in prayer.' Then the angel instructed him in the need for chains of prayer services, stressed that he had fourteen days and told him: 'Go to the highest authority if it is necessary.' Johan was overwhelmed and almost struck dumb with the awesome presence. But how could he take the message to the whole country? He would be laughed out of court. He made excuses, saying, 'I shall cry if I have to recount what is happening to me now.' The angel replied, 'What are a few tears compared to rivers of blood, my son?'

After the angel left, Johan wrestled in prayer for several hours. When he realized that fourteen days later was 6 April, which was Founders' Day in South Africa, Johan decided that he was prepared to go to any lengths to share the angel's message. He took his story to President de Clerk, who took his account seriously and encouraged him to call for more prayer, especially on Founders' Day. His testimony gave great impetus to a Day of National Prayer which even the newspapers regarded as a crucial factor in the peaceful outcome of the elections.

Such days of prayer have restarted in South Africa, mainly praying for community transformation and a revival of Spirit-led Christianity. By 2005 their influence had spread to many African countries and even to the much more secular climate in Europe.

Mark Stibbe, now vicar of St Andrew's, Chorleywood, which is one of the largest Anglican churches in England, had a remarkable conversion when a pupil at Winchester College[2]. A few years later, having just begun at university, his conversion was sealed in a remarkable way. He writes:

A visitor in the Cathedral Close

In the Christmas holidays of 1980, I was struggling with my faith. I was enjoying my new-found freedom as an undergraduate, while at the same time trying to live the Christian life. As a result, I was wrestling with the issues of commitment and compromise.

At the height of my inner turmoil, I remember going to bed one night feeling very restless. At the time, I was staying at my parents' house in Norwich Cathedral Close. I remember shutting the door, and then retiring. I always shut my bedroom door as a matter of routine; my mother kept a rather large Siamese cat that used to come into my room uninvited.

I woke up at six minutes past one in the morning. My digital alarm clock revealed the time. I was definitely awake not sleeping. The next moment the bedroom door flew open very quickly. Strangely, it did not crash against the wardrobe next to it, but came very suddenly to a halt, a very few centimetres away from it.

What happened next will remain with me for the rest of my life. In walked a tall, white, radiant figure, about seven or eight feet in height. I looked towards the face but there were no definable features. The light was simply too bright for me to make out any discernible features. But I knew it was a face.

For a few seconds, the angelic being stood before me. I was not at all frightened. A hand reached out to me, beckoning. I heard the words, 'Follow me.' Then the figure left. Needless to say, I was greatly impacted by the event. I told my parents the next morning. They could see that I was in a state of shock. They were unusually receptive. As a result of what I took to be a visit from the angel of the Lord, I decided that day to live the rest of my life completely for Jesus Christ. Though I have had times of weakness and wilderness since then, my heart has been wholly for the Lord. The days of divided loyalties ended there and then.

Since then, Mark has developed one of the most effective theological, pastoral and evangelistic ministries in the modern Anglican Church.

Powerful protection

Jackie Pullinger, author of *Chasing the Dragon*, is well known for her extraordinary work amongst the drug addicts of the Walled City in Hong Kong. I would imagine her guardian angel has to work overtime! But this is a story from England (sent to me by my friend Elizabeth Brazell who leads The Word for the Life Trust):

In the late 1990s Jackie Pullinger was speaking at a mission in the Winter Garden in Blackpool. There had been a great deal of spiritual warfare and deliverance amongst those who had come to the Lord that week. I was working with one of the teams of prayer intercessors for the last evening. Our role was to walk round the building, in pairs, praying. My prayer partner and I sat down at the top level on the steps, very weary after about 8 hours of prayer, ministry and mission work!

Jackie was giving her final talk of the mission – I looked at the stage – on either side of her were two huge angels; they seemed at least three times as tall as her therefore about 15 to 16 feet tall. They each had swords of light in *their left hands* which were raised in an arch above her head as she preached. The angels seemed to be made of some metallic substance, not hard but fluid and shining, the light around them was glorious – I realised that others could not see them, but I wondered about my prayer partner – so I asked her 'Can you see what I see?'

Her reply was, 'I don't know what you can see but I can see two angels looking after Jackie, – with swords *in their left hands*! I guess she'll be OK for a little time'

Quite why Jackie needed this powerful protection is unclear. But angels are often seen when effective prayer is taking place. The detail about the swords in the *left hand* of the angels is fascinating – totally unexpected and yet seen by two independent witnesses!

Distressed parent
Fran Hawkins, also a leader in The Word for the Life Trust, sent me this story.

It took place during a mission in Wales in the mid 1990s. Two people were praying for healing with someone who had miscarried two babies some ten years previously. As they prayed, in an upper room in a church in the town centre, they saw an angel. Here is their testimony given in October 1995:

At about 9 p.m. the room filled with light and all three of us stopped praying and looked towards the light. There was an angel standing in the corner of the room, light, shining, very tall, silver/gold colour. He reached down to the lady who was receiving ministry and she was able to see that in his arms was a tiny baby girl. He showed the baby and then carrying it very carefully faded from sight. We knew without doubt that the baby had been the first miscarried baby which had been taken by the angel to God. The baby had just been named Grace by her mother – A huge peace came over us all especially the one receiving ministry. All three of us testified to seeing the angel and when we shared descriptions they were very similar.

It was particularly wonderful that the distressed mother, who was being prayed for, also saw the angel. She will have received the double reassurance of God's peace for herself and her lost baby.

Angels as unrecognized helpers

Unexpected helpers in Northern Nigeria
Baroness Cox was preaching at Christchurch Clifton on the evening of Remembrance Sunday in November 2002. In the midst of a powerful and moving sermon about the courage, faith and graciousness of the persecuted church in Southern Sudan, Northern Nigeria, Indonesia and in Nagorno Karabakh (part of the ancient Christian Kingdom of Armenia) she included the following story:

> She was travelling from Kaduna, in Northern Nigeria, to Abuja, to catch a plane home. The flight was important; not only were their tickets non-refundable, but also she was due to speak in an important debate on Africa in the House of Lords the very next day. As often when travelling in Africa, there was little time to spare. About a hundred miles from the airport, in the midst of typical African bush, they met another vehicle which flashed its lights at them. They ground to a halt, and the other car swept on its journey.
>
> They got out, wondering what was wrong. The ominous sight of oil gushing out from the rear wheel greeted them. None of them had mechanical skills, and they held a quick prayer meeting on the now deserted road. Out of the bush, two strong, and competent, young men appeared. Within two minutes, they had opened the back, extracted some tools, and taken the wheel off – no mean feat! But the travellers' joy was short lived. As the wheel was being removed, bearings hurtled out in all directions.
>
> Another brief prayer meeting was held. Suddenly, a

young boy aged about twelve appeared. He was carrying a black plastic bag, containing a supply of new wheel bearings, all designed to fit a Honda vehicle! The wheel, and its bearings, was restored, and they were instructed to test drive the car. It immediately became apparent that another wheel needed the same treatment. Help came as before, and they were able to continue their journey after a delay of a mere twenty minutes. Baroness Cox remarked, 'Where in Bristol could you get back on the road after twenty minutes if the wheel bearings had gone?'

The travellers had received a truly miraculous answer to prayer! Probably we shouldn't try to analyse these sorts of experiences. God's sovereign hand was clearly at work. Personally, having experienced much travel in Africa and the difficulty of sorting out repairs when vehicles break down, I find the explanation that the little boy was a 'guardian angel' far more probable than the natural one of an unexpected human intervention!

The main thrust of her sermon, and in the book about some of her work[3] was of the amazing grace given to the beleaguered Christians in so many different situations. She also believes (and there is much in Scripture to support this, particularly in the searching parable of the sheep and the goats, Matthew 25:31–46) that God expects his church in the comfortable West to do far more by prayer, and by practical and political action, to support their brothers and sisters in adversity.

As we shall see throughout the book, such stories of unexpected helpers are reasonably common. In most cases, the simplest, and most plausible, explanation is to accept that the help that people received was from angels; even if it was through human intervention, they all received remarkable help and/or protection.

This, however, raises a familiar dilemma: If God helps Baroness Cox on a journey to an airport, where is the help for the persecuted communities which she is working so valiantly to help?

This is a really troubling question. We cannot expect to fully understand God's sovereign will. In the experience of the early church, James (second in all the Gospel lists of apostles) was martyred by King Herod, while Peter was released from Herod's prison by an angel[4]. Unless God has ordained a clockwork universe where there is no possibility of accident, natural disaster, sin or spiritual opposition, such outcomes are inevitable. We have to be prepared to live with this uncertainty – otherwise we will have to abandon any concept of a God who intervenes.

The next two stories come from Pat, a new friend, who has suffered much from ill health over the years, but who is used much by God in praying for other people (see page 185). These two events have helped her to trust God for miracles when she prays for others. In one the angel comes, unrecognized, as a human helper, in the second the bright light and the miraculous escape are characteristic of angelic intervention:

> I used to drive one of those awful invalid carriages – blue fibreglass, three wheels and very unreliable. I was 22 years old and in my first job. It was early spring. I had spent the weekend with my parents and set off for work on Monday morning. I was driving through a small

village when the engine cut out. I tried to start it, but nothing worked. It was about 7.30 a.m.

I looked around. There were fields immediately on my left, sloping up and away from the road. On my right was a small row of houses and then fields. I needed help. I decided to knock at one of the houses and ask if I could use a telephone (this was in the days before mobile phones). In order to get out of the car, I had to push the door away from me and slide it backwards. I pushed the door but it would not slide, it was completely stuck. I pulled and pushed for a couple of minutes but it would not move. I tried the other door which opened correctly, but I couldn't get out that side because there was no pavement, only grass that sloped up and away from me.

I looked around again. There was no one in sight. I prayed, 'Lord Jesus, please help me.' I sat looking out of the window for several minutes, wondering how the Lord would answer me.

On my left, over the fields in the distance, a man appeared. He was walking too far away for me to call him, so I just watched. As he drew closer I realised he would not pass close enough for me to ask for his help. I kept watching him. He changed direction slightly and came towards me. He was about my age and was wearing a dark blue and light blue checked shirt, open at the neck with sleeves rolled up to the elbows, denim dungarees and black work boots. He walked straight up to the car and before I could say anything, he slid the door rearwards with the greatest of ease.

I got out of the car and said, 'Thank you.' Praise the Lord was on my lips, but no sooner had I said, 'Thank you' than there was the sound of a car horn behind me.

I looked around and there was a lady leaning out of her car asking if I needed any help. I said, 'This gentleman has just helped me get out of the car...' 'What gentleman?' she interrupted. 'This one,' I said turning back to him... and he was not there. I had only turned my head for a second or two and he was gone. I looked all around and there was no sign of him at all. The lady offered me the use of her telephone and I was able to call work, the garage and my sister to collect me.

Later that day I thought about events. The young man was immaculately presented – clean and shiny black hair in a long pudding basin cut, his clothing was immaculate and looked new and pressed, his boots were shiny (after walking over the fields, not a trace of mud on them!). I hadn't said what help I needed. He didn't ask – he didn't speak to me at all. He disappeared as soon as I was distracted.

I did not hear about angels in human form until several years later. When I read about how the Lord sends them to help us, I knew he had sent an angel *that day* – I have never forgotten.

Later that year, in winter, I was making the same journey through the same village one lunchtime. There was snow covering the road and it was packed hard where cars had been over it, leaving a ridge in the middle of the tyre tracks. I approached a bend in the road where there were huge trees growing and the trunks reached almost to the roadside. As I turned into the bend, the single front wheel skidded off the snow packed ridge and I lost control of the car.

The trees loomed large in my windscreen as I struggled in vain to control the car. I thought my life was over.

I shut my eyes and prayed, 'Help me, Lord. You and I may be seeing each other face to face in a minute. Have mercy on me.' I waited for the impact, knowing the fibreglass would crumple. A very bright light surrounded me, like the sun coming out from behind a cloud and shining directly on me, but much brighter; even with my eyes closed, I was aware of the light for several seconds. No impact came.

The presence of the Lord was so strong, I wondered if I had been spared the pain of death and gone straight to heaven. I didn't dare open my eyes and asked the Lord what I should do. He said gently, 'Open your eyes.' I did. The landscape was familiar, snow, fields, houses, but no trees. I looked in the rear view mirror and the trees were behind me. The car was facing 180 degrees from where I had been and I was about twenty yards away, parked perfectly, the engine still running, next to the row of houses. There were no skid marks, no tracks in the snow and not a mark on the car. It was as if the Lord had sent angels to pluck me off the road and put me out of danger. I believe they did just that! I drove off – my heart singing to the Lord as I went.

Angels who provided protection in times of extreme danger

There are many stories of angelic protection both of individuals and of groups of people. Throughout this book, this theme will reoccur. Corrie Ten Boom[5], herself a miraculous survivor of a German concentration camp, was certainly familiar with the work of angels. She tells of an event during a rebellion in the Congo. This short story is typical, and has a biblical parallel (see below) in 2 Kings 6 when Elisha is protected from a powerful enemy force sent to take him prisoner. Here a group of rebels, in one of the many Congo uprisings, advanced on a school where 200 children of missionaries lived. She writes:

> They had planned to kill both children and teachers. In the school, they knew the danger, and therefore went to prayer. Their only protection was a fence and a couple of soldiers; while the enemy, who came closer and closer, numbered several hundreds. When the rebels were close by, suddenly something happened. They turned and ran away! The same thing happened on each of the next two days. One of the rebels was wounded, and he was brought into the missionary hospital. When the doctor was dressing his wounds, he asked the soldier, 'Why did you not break into the school as you had planned?' The soldier replied, 'We couldn't do it; we saw hundreds of soldiers in white uniforms, and we became scared.' Of course, in Africa soldiers do not wear white uniforms.

Corrie concluded,

> They must have been angels. What a wonderful thing that the Lord can open the eyes of the enemy so that they see angels!

No one can fully understand the appropriate spiritual conditions for this sort of intervention; but the evidence that such events do from time to time occur is overwhelming (see Chapter 3 especially for more examples).

Divine protection and worshipping angels in Bougainville

In the 1990s there was very violent rebellion in Bougainville, a large island to the NE of Papua New Guinea. Times were very dangerous, many people were killed and Christians had a very difficult time. As so often in these situations, there were also many remarkable stories of God's protection and of his angels. Here are a few examples supplied by my friends Conrad and Phyllis Hurd who have spent much of their life translating the Scriptures into local languages in Bougainville:

When the people, who were faced with hardship, sought the Lord in prayer and took cover in his name, many extraordinary things happened. Two local pastors, Micah and Penias testified:

Armed men would spray innocent men with automatic fire, but the bullets simply fell from their bodies like rain, while the jungle on either side would be scythed to the ground. Those who had taken part in violence, did not receive as much protection. Occasionally, God would give them warnings by allowing them to escape death with minor injuries. After two warnings, however, those who didn't repent usually received further injuries that proved fatal.

Samuel Meekera is a minister of the gospel, a member of the United Church. He had some parishioners who were members of the revolutionary forces. They believed that they had the right to rob and pillage the property of those who had fled from the island because of the crisis. He preached, fearlessly, about the need for honesty. Eventually, the revolutionaries had heard enough. One of them pointed his M-16 at him and fired from a range of ten yards. The tracer bullet popped out of the muzzle and landed spluttering in the dirt between them. The gunman fired again. This time the gun roared but the bullet missed. Impressed by what seemed to be divine protection, the soldier made no further attempts to kill Samuel and the revolutionaries in that area began to have a special respect for the Christian leaders.

John Wesley Kitare lived in the village of Sinare. His wife was at home when helicopters attacked their village in a pre-dawn raid. When his wife saw the hail of fire, she rebuked it in the name of the Lord! As the helicopter swept by, the villagers testified that they saw the tracers visibly diverted away from them.

At the same time, there was a raid on nearby Roreinang. Roreinang is a former Methodist Mission Station which is now run by the indigenous church. It has a superintendent minister, a large elementary school and a conference centre for the church in southern Bougainville. In 1997, the Defence Force started an operation to overrun the Siang and Aropa valleys. The plan was to rout the enemy, even if every village in the area was destroyed in the process. Roreinang was one of the villages designated for a destructive attack.

Ministers from the whole area were just finishing a prayer conference, when helicopters carrying automatic weapons and grenade launchers made a pre-dawn raid. The acting bishop, Meshac Tarurava, jumped out of bed with a strange feeling of militant joy. He said 'No hiding place is safe, but God is our refuge. Call out to him!' He then went out and stood in the middle of a nearby sweet potato patch, lifted his hands towards heaven and forbade the bullets and the grenades to do any damage to the Mission Station.

The helicopter circled the station three or four times spraying bullets and launching grenades, but not a single person or dwelling was hit! Later when Meshac sent people out to assess the damage, no one could find a trace of bullet holes or any sort of damage.

Visions of angels became quite common during these times. Usually they were seen and heard worshipping God. Their presence was always accompanied by a wonderful aroma (see 2 Corinthians 2:14–17). Sometimes only some people could see them, at others times the only indication of their presence was the fragrance[6].

The ministers who spoke to Conrad and Phyllis impressed them with the great awe with which they spoke about these supernatural matters. A typical comment was:

Sometimes the angels would come when we were conducting family worship and they would sing along with our families! They would appear out of nowhere and sing to us and we would join them! They could appear anywhere – they even appeared in the church here in Arawa. They stood behind me (Micah) while I was preaching. The children saw the angels and told me about them!

The angels always inspired people to worship the Lord. We would sing and worship for hours upon end in their presence. We never got tired! *Now the crisis is over, these kinds of things don't happen anymore, I really miss them!* The sweetest days of my life were those that I had experiencing the presence of God in the midst of the terrible crisis.

Certainly, angelic experiences seem more common in places where believers are in great danger.

An angel in a dream

Before the troubles, Meshac Tarurava, then a minister in the Methodist Church in Papua New Guinea, helped my friends Conrad and Phyllis Hurd with Bible translation in Bougainville. In the late 1970s, his church had purchased a Land Cruiser and he had charge of it. The clutch failed. Mesach went and purchased a new one – even though he didn't know how he was going to get it installed! He had spent all the available money on the parts and couldn't employ a mechanic (even if one had been available!).

Before he went to sleep, he prayed and asked God for directions as to how to put the new clutch in. That night, in a dream, a little man came to him and said 'I've come to show you how to install the clutch, so that you will be able to do it yourself!'

Meshac understood that the little man was an angel, because this is how angels usually look in Bougainville. He watched carefully as the angel took out the old clutch and replaced it with a new one.

In the morning, with his heart full of joy, Meshac collected the tools that he would need and precisely followed the angelic instructions! He fixed it without any problems, praising God for sending his angel to show him how to do a very necessary practical task.

I must confess that not even angelic instruction would persuade your author that he could fit a clutch!

Angels at conferences and places of worship

Many people have heard angels singing. There are accounts from churches and conferences from all over the world. Hope Price[7] writes:

> Many people, including my family and myself, have heard the magnificence of angelic singing on cassette tape! Four members of a worship group in Surrey were practising a chorus 'Alleluiah, Alleluiah' in an otherwise empty church. They recorded what their little group had sung with guitar accompaniment but, when they played back the tape, they were staggered to hear hundreds of voices singing. To all who heard this, it is a wondrous sound, which makes us glorify God. The descants are much higher than human voices can reach and the harmonies are so intricate; it makes truly thrilling listening.

In an earlier book[8], I recorded in detail an incident from the Chinese underground church in 1995, when in Shandong people were singing in tongues. The singing was recorded, and when the tape was played it was overlaid with the sound of angels singing a song in Mandarin which no one had heard to a musical accompaniment that had not been there. It is rather wonderful that a small music group, in the safety of a church in Surrey, should have the same experience as a persecuted group in China.

My favourite example of angels at conferences comes

from Penny Phillips. We had met, for the first time, about eighteen months earlier at the baptism of one of her grandchildren. Penny was interested that I written about angels, and we became firm friends. She was already seriously ill with leukemia.

As a result of much prayer from many people, her illness progressed quite slowly and many good things happened in the last two years of her life. My final conversation with her, on the phone, was again about angels. She, now desperately ill, was concerned to help me with a new project. Her only desire was to bring glory to God in whatever way she could, and I for one am deeply grateful to have known her. Her vision of heaven, her faith, her courage and her sense of humour were a wonderful antidote to any gloom and self-pity! This is what she shared:

I was leading a series of creative arts seminars at New Wine. I, and my co-leader, were quite depressed by how it was going. We prayed, with great intensity, with one of the conference leaders. We felt the atmosphere in the tent lift. During the seminar, we were aware of a rustling of wings. A number of the participants heard the same phenomena. During the sharing time, at the end of the day, many of those present became aware of the presence of the angels. The adults felt wings brushing them, as though feathers were touching their shoulders.

Afterwards, they started, in amazement, to share what they had experienced. As the adults shared, the children who were present (quite a small number) said 'But didn't you see them?' They then described the angels splashed with the colours of the rainbow and gold. Some children who were present drew pictures of angels which they said they had seen. The seminar helped release a number of people from fears and anxieties; it also inspired some to new levels of creativity.

A lovely story, told to me by a lovely person, just a few days before she died. It was deeply moving that someone so near to death could be so concerned to help someone else!

Angels in the Bible – What do they look like?[9]

Matthew describes the angel beside the tomb on the first Easter morning as follows: 'His appearance was like lightning, and his clothes were white as snow' (Matthew 28:3) which fits with the traditional view of what angels look like. The Bible seldom describes the appearance of angels or other supernatural beings.

The Bible gives many examples of encounters with angels. There are over 600 references in its pages! The most well known are the visit of the angel Gabriel to Mary (Luke 1:26–38) and the company of angels speaking and singing to God and the shepherds (Luke 2:8–20) – the subject of many unconvincing Nativity plays, which may help to promote scepticism about things angelic! These two encounters, and the majority of those in Scripture, feature what we may presume to be 'traditional' angels. The Bible speaks of glory (Luke 2:9) and immense brightness (Daniel 10:6). These features help to authenticate the angelic visitation.

Angels, and indeed God himself, do sometimes appear incognito; most notably in the appearance to Samson's parents (Judges 13) and in the appearance of three visitors to Abraham (Genesis 18). The writer of the letter to the

Hebrews (Hebrews 13:2), referring back to Genesis 18 encourages hospitality with the words 'Do not forget to entertain strangers, for by so doing some people have entertained angels *without knowing it*' (my italics).

The two disciples who walked to Emmaus on the first Easter Day *failed to recognize* the risen Lord until the moment before he disappeared from their sight (Luke 24:31). Abraham (Genesis 18 and Hebrews 13:2) failed to recognize who his visitors were. Thus it is hardly surprising that people today encounter angels without realizing the significance of their meetings – *at least until sometime afterwards!*

Angels do bring protection and are sometimes unseen by those in trouble. In 2 Kings 6, neither Elisha's servant nor the Arameans who had been sent to capture Elisha were aware of the supernatural protection that the Lord had provided for Elisha. Daniel (Daniel 6:22) was protected by an angel in the lion's den; his companions Shadrach, Meshach and Abednego were visited by an angel who protected them from the fiery furnace (Daniel 3:25) who was, possibly, only seen by the king.

In the Bible, angels also appear in dreams, visions and at times of worship. Jacob's ladder (Genesis 28:10–19) is a famous example. Isaiah had a profound experience when worshipping in the temple (see Isaiah 6). In the Revelation of John, written during or after a visionary experience, angels are heard worshipping God (Revelation 4 and in many other places).

Scripture also gives plenty of warnings about false angelic experiences and the book of Revelation suggests that when Satan fell a third of the angels in heaven fell with him (see Revelation 12:4). We shall look at this side of the angelic experience in Chapters 8 and 9. Returning to the examples cited in this chapter and throughout the book, we need to ask a crucial question:

Are these experiences from God?

There are two other possible explanations. They may be a form of self-delusion or they may be a serious spiritual deception. Self-delusion is obviously a possibility. Some people have vivid imaginations, and in some situations (such as rather ecstatic Christian conferences), they may even be trying to keep with the spiritual Joneses!

Genuine angelic experiences are usually *unsought* (it is appropriate in some situations to pray for angelic protection – which is promised in Psalm 91:11 and Psalm 34:7); false experiences are likely to occur where people have been taught to rely on spirit guides, guardian angels and other spiritual beings who can be summoned almost at will.

We are warned in the Bible that there is the very real possibility of being deceived. We live in a very credulous age. Many people are actively seeking, and being encouraged to seek, supernatural experiences. Most popular books on angels actively encourage their readers to seek, to visualize, or even create angels. All of this is very different from the sober teachings of Scripture.

'Angels of light' (deceiving spirits – fallen angels) appear as spirit guides or purport to be angels sent from God who seem reassuring but actually give guidance which is contrary to biblical teaching and which ensnares people in a cycle of false and dangerous experiences. People quite often experience evil spirits, ghosts or poltergeists, which are all an obvious part of the fallen spiritual world. Although such

encounters can be very frightening, they are easier to deal
with and to discern than the 'angels of light' (see 2
Corinthians 11:14) who with persuasive subtlety pretend to
be God's messengers.

There is one safe test – given by Jesus: 'By their fruit you
will recognise them' (Matthew 7:20). Jesus is actually talking about the difference between true and false prophets.
The same test applies to true and false angels.

If the fruit of an 'angelic' encounter is good, if someone's
faith is strengthened, if their life is changed, if Jesus' name
is glorified, then the encounter is likely to have been genuine. If the result is spiritual confusion, if the guidance or
instructions are contrary to the teaching of Scripture, if the
result brings glory to some human or 'angelic' agency, then
the encounter is not from God.

It should be possible to apply these tests to all the stories
in this, or any other, book on the subject.

Summary

The accounts that I have cited earlier in the chapter, all have
parallels in Scripture. In each of them there was a positive
spiritual result. Angels do not appear for some private glory
trip, nor are they conjured up by some psychic experience;
they appear as God's messengers to instruct, to guide, to
protect and to warn. Sometimes, angels are sensed or heard
during the worship of God. This is to be expected as worship is a significant part of their divine purpose according
to the pages of Scripture!

Notes

1. Michael Cassidy, *A Witness For Ever*, London: Hodder & Stoughton, 1995, p. 160.
2. Mark Stibbe, *Thinking Clearly about Revival*, Oxford: Monarch, 1998, p. 24. A number of others who came to faith at this time are serving God in full-time Christian work.
3. Baroness Cox is a well-known member of the House of Lords, who campaigns fearlessly on behalf of many Third World, and other Christian causes. I am grateful to two of my children who heard the sermon for drawing my attention to it! See also, Andrew Boyd, *Baroness Cox – a Voice for the Voiceless*, Oxford: Lion, 1998.
4. See Acts 12:1–17.
5. Corrie Ten Boom, *Marching Orders for the End Battle*, Fort Washington, 1960, p. 89f.
6. See Bilquis Sheikh, *I dared to call him Father*, E. Sussex: Kingsway, 1998 for a beautiful account of this sort of fragrance (pp. 26–35).
7. Hope Price, *Angels*, London: Pan Books, 1994, p. 70ff.
8. John Woolmer, *Angels*, Oxford: Monarch, 2003, pp. 158–161.
9. For a much more detailed biblical account, see John Woolmer, *Angels*, Chapters 2 and 3.

Chapter 3

Angels Who Protect and Help

IN THIS CHAPTER, we look at the role of angels as protectors of people who are in deep trouble. There are many accounts of this type of experience both in recent history and in the Bible. While many modern accounts of angelic intervention can seem quite trivial, the situations described here were very serious. This seems in line with many of the situations described in the Bible.

The Heavenly Man

During the 1990s, we occasionally heard rumours of what God was doing in China. The reality far exceeded what most of us could have expected. One of the most remarkable leaders of the underground church was Brother Yun, who was given the nickname 'the Heavenly Man'.

In the autumn of 2004 in Leicester, I listened to the testimonies of two of the most gracious Christian men that I have ever met. Brother Yun, well known as the author of *The Heavenly Man*, and Brother Xu were both members of the Chinese house church movement. Both men had suffered a great deal for their faith.

They are now living in the West and deeply committed to spreading their faith especially in the old route between

China and Jerusalem which takes them through many countries which are hostile to their faith. In Leicester, it was very moving to see them pray for at least fifty Chinese university students, many of whom would have come from a background which would have been very opposed to their mission work in China.

Twice Yun escaped from prison in a way reminiscent of Peter in Acts 12. The first occasion was in 1983. The house church, especially around Henan in central China, was growing. The leaders had a fantastic dedication to the Lord, often expressed in fasting and prayer. At one prayer meeting, Yun experienced spiritual warfare at first hand.[1]

Before we left for Shaanxi that evening we asked God to prepare the hearts of the people to receive his Word. While praying, I suddenly saw a terrible vision that shook my soul. The others told me I startled them when I shouted out, 'Hallelujah! Jesus' blood has overcome you!'

Everybody stopped praying and asked me what the matter was. With sweat on my brow I told them, 'I saw a terrible evil vision. A black, heinous creature came after me. It had a horrible twisted face. It pressed me down on the ground and sat on my stomach so I couldn't get up. With one of its hands it grabbed my throat and started choking me. With its other hand it grabbed some steel pliers and tried to shut my mouth with them. I could hardly breathe. Then I saw a great strong angel fly toward me. With all my strength I poked my fingers into the eyes of the evil creature. It fell to the ground, and I was carried away to safety by the angel. I shouted, 'Hallelujah! Jesus' blood has overcome you!'

Soon afterwards, Yun was arrested. He was dragged through the streets, paraded bloody and bruised, through a town in a way that reminded him of the experience of the apostles (see 1 Corinthians 4:9). Back in prison, he felt that God was calling him to escape.

Many spectators had crowded outside the prison window and looked in. One officer went to another room and made a telephone call to Henan, to try and find out who I was from the authorities there. The other interrogators went with him to hear what was said. They left me alone in the room and shut the door. I was still tightly bound by rope, so they saw no chance I could escape. The onlookers also gave their attention to the telephone call, and crowded outside the window of that room to listen.

At that moment, with everyone's eyes off me, the Holy Spirit spoke to my heart, 'The God of Peter is your God.' I remembered how angels had opened the prison gates for Peter to escape. 'Are not all angels ministering spirits sent to serve those who will inherit salvation?' (Hebrews 1:14)

The rope that bound my arms behind my back suddenly snapped by itself!

I walked through the middle of the onlookers in the courtyard. Nobody stopped me or said anything to me! It was as though God had blinded their eyes and they didn't recognise who I was.

Because the front gates had been locked, the only way out of the compound was over an eight-foot high cement wall. The wall had sharp glass embedded in the top.

First I pulled myself up onto the wall as high as I could manage. I looked over the top and saw that on the other side was a ten feet wide, open septic tank. As I hung grimly onto the side of the wall, all of a sudden, I felt as if somebody hoisted me up and threw me over! I jumped so far that I even cleared the septic tank!

Yun believes the same angel he saw in his vision lifted him up. He completed his escape, and continued to minister to the hidden house churches of his district and further afield. He had many extraordinary adventures, arrests, imprisonments, and suffered terrible torture. His testimony reads very like Paul's in 2 Corinthians 11:16ff.

His final imprisonment in China was in Zhengzhou maximum security prison in Henan. As usual, he was tortured, and on this occasion, he had to be carried around the prison by friends, as his legs had been broken. He felt very discouraged, and constantly cried out to the Lord. On 4 May 1997, God intervened dramatically. First, he was given a severe warning and a great promise of freedom from Jeremiah 15:19–21. Then he had a powerful vision, even though he was wide awake. He saw his wife, just released from prison, binding his wounds and preparing medicine. In the vision, she said to him, 'Why don't you open the iron door?' Before he could reply, she walked out of the room, and the vision ended. He heard the Lord say, 'This is the hour of your salvation.'

A fellow believer, Xu, who had carried him around the prison twice said, 'Yun, you must escape.' It was completely impossible. Apart from his broken legs, his escape involved passing through three normally locked doors, walking across a large courtyard, and out through the main gate, onto a busy street. But after so many different signs, he knew that he had to attempt the impossible.

He describes in great detail what happened. He was able

to pass through the first gate because a prisoner came in the opposite direction, and the guard was distracted by a phone call. The second and third gates, unaccountably, were open and he walked past guards who seemed totally unaware of his presence.

He walked across the courtyard (not realizing until later that his broken legs had been healed), and the main gate was open! A taxi drew up outside, and he was able to direct the driver to the house of some believers. The believers, unlike those praying for Peter's release, were expecting him, as was his wife. The authorities failed to find him; they were hindered by a huge rainstorm just as they discovered his escape! Eventually he escaped from China with a false passport, including a photograph to which he bore no resemblance.

Although there were no discernible angels in his second escape, the way he walked past the security guards and the unexpectedly open gates is very similar to Acts 12:10.

Brother Xu's confirmation of the story
This remarkable testimony was confirmed by Brother Xu. Xu was also in the prison in Henan. He was in solitary confinement, allowed out occasionally to assist Yun (who couldn't walk) by taking him to the toilet and to wash. Xu and Yun, although both leaders of the church, seldom managed to meet – usually one or the other was in prison!

On the morning of 4 May 1997, Xu heard what he understood to be the voice of God. He was lying on his bed, locked in his cell. The voice told him to get up, leave the cell, and tell Yun that it was time for him to escape. Not surprisingly, Xu was very frightened. He got up, and to his amazement, the prison door opened. He walked into the corridor and was so scared that he returned to his cell and closed the door (which of course relocked it). He lay down on his bed.

The voice spoke a second time. Again he got up, again the door was unlocked. This time he found Yun and gave him God's message. Xu returned to his cell and came back with his towel and toothbrush to give the impression that they were going to wash. He repeated his message 'Yun, you must escape!' Xu took Yun to the first door, and then returned to his cell.

He hid under the mattress and prayed desperately for Yun's protection. He also prayed for cover for Yun's escape. Shortly after Yun had reached safety, a torrential rainstorm made all pursuit by the authorities much more difficult. Xu was kept in prison for many years, but eventually found his way to the West.

In John 12:28 we are told that Jesus heard a voice from heaven 'I have glorified it, and will glorify it again'. The crowd that was there and heard it said it had thundered; another said an angel had spoken to him. The voice of God and the voices of angels must be similar! Yun's escape, Xu's voice and the unlocked doors and gates, indicate much divine activity on 4 May! All of which was not very different from something that occurred in Jerusalem sometime around AD 35.

Peter's escape from Herod's prison

… Peter was kept in prison, but the church was earnestly praying to God for him.

The night before Herod was to bring him to trial, Peter was sleeping between two soldiers, bound with two chains, and sentries stood guard at the entrance.

Suddenly an angel of the Lord appeared and a light shone in the cell. He struck Peter on the side and woke him up. 'Quick, get up!' he said, and the chains fell off Peter's wrists.

Then the angel said to him, 'Put on your clothes and sandals.' And Peter did so. 'Wrap your cloak around you and follow me,' the angel told him. Peter followed him out of the prison, but he had no idea that what the angel was doing was really happening; he thought he was seeing a vision. They passed the first and second guards and came to the iron gate leading to the city. It opened for them by itself, and they went through it. When they had walked the length of one street, suddenly the angel left him.

Then Peter came to himself and said, 'Now I know without a doubt that the Lord sent his angel and rescued me from Herod's clutches and from everything the Jewish people were anticipating.'

When this had dawned on him, he went to the house of Mary the mother of John, also called Mark, where many people had gathered and were praying. Peter knocked at the outer entrance, and a servant girl named Rhoda came to answer the door. When she recognised Peter's voice, she was so overjoyed she ran back without opening it and exclaimed, 'Peter is at the door!'

'You're out of your mind,' they told her. When she kept insisting that it was so, they said, *'It must be his angel.'*

But Peter kept on knocking, and when they opened the door and saw him, they were astonished. Peter motioned with his hand for them to be quiet and described how the Lord had brought him out of prison.

'Tell James and the brothers about this,' he said, and then he left for another place.

In the morning, there was no small commotion among the soldiers as to what had become of Peter. After Herod had a thorough search made for him and did not find him, he cross-examined the guards and ordered that they be executed. (Acts 12:5–19, my italics)

It is very interesting that the believers told Rhoda that the voice she had heard was *Peter's angel*. This shows that the early church believed in guardian angels, which was also the belief of the Jewish rabbis at the time. It also shows how the early Christians, like most of us, find it hard to believe that God has answered our prayers!

Guardian angels and the Bible

In Jesus' life, the question of guardian angels arose both in the temptation narrative, and in the Garden of Gethsemane. On one occasion, Jesus indirectly mentioned guardian angels:

See that you do not look down on one of these little ones. For I tell you that their angels in heaven always see the face of my Father in heaven.

What do you think? If a man owns a hundred sheep, and one of them wanders away, will he not leave the ninety-nine on the hills and go and look for the one that wandered off? And if he finds it, I tell you the truth, he is happier about that one sheep than about the ninety-nine that did not wander off. In the same way, your Father in heaven is not willing that any of these little ones should be lost. (Matthew 18:10–14)

What Jesus meant by 'their angels in heaven' has been much discussed. Commentators are uncertain as to how literally to take the reference to angels. Their views usually reflect their own theological presuppositions. The Old Testament, which was Jesus' reference book, is very clear: Psalm 91:11–12 tells us of God's protection (for those that trust him):

For He will command his angels concerning you to guard you in all your ways; they will lift you up in their hands, so that you will not strike your foot against a stone.

Psalm 34:7 is even stronger:

The angel of the LORD encamps around those who fear him, and he delivers them.

The book of Daniel has a number of angelic incidents, notably in Daniel 6:21 when Daniel accounts for his preservation from the lions by telling the king, 'My God sent his angel, and he shut the mouths of the lions.'

In view of these texts, I think that Jesus intended his teaching to be understood literally! In which case, children (see especially the end of the next chapter), and the child-like in faith, have protective angels! However, the existence of guardian angels *does not guarantee* protection. It does imply that God cares and is concerned for all the little ones – children, ordinary believers...

Earlier in his Gospel, Matthew has recorded the grim story of the massacre of the innocents (Matthew 2:16–18).

This ghastly story, together with the pages of human history, show all too clearly that such protection is not automatic. Indeed, it cannot be unless we have a universe in which evil is eliminated. It may have been some slight comfort to the grieving mothers in Bethlehem, prophesied by Jeremiah 31:15, if they were able to believe that their children were now in the presence of the Lord.

We continue with some other stories of guardian angels which illustrate the different ways in which they come to help. The evidence for their presence is very strong; the mystery is when they are permitted to act and when they have to stay their protective hands.

Protection for a missionary

Revd John Paton[2] was an intrepid missionary to the New Hebrides. He suffered much persecution and hardship, but eventually saw a lot of fruit for his labours. On one occasion, in the 1860s, hostile natives surrounded his headquarters. John and his wife prayed all night for protection; they were alone and defenceless – only God could help them. When daylight came, they were amazed, and relieved, to see the attackers leave.

Years later, the tribe's chief became a Christian. Mr Paton asked him why he and his followers hadn't burnt the house down. The chief explained that he had seen many hundreds of men, in shining garments, standing with drawn swords, circling the mission station. They were far too afraid to attack. Only then did John Paton realize that God had sent his angels to protect him and his wife.

This story is typical of many accounts of angels

providing protection, which *is unseen by those in trouble*, but which causes attackers to withdraw and leave their intended victims in safety.

Protection in China, stories in Winchester

Winchester Cathedral seems a beautifully safe place. Impeccable singing, marvellous architecture and sensible orthodox Anglican worship combine with a deep sense of history and beauty, to soothe rather than to challenge.

Jane Austen lies buried on the northern side of the nave. St Swithin, of rain-making fame lies, finally undisturbed, just outside the walls. Izaak Walton, theologian and fisherman extraordinaire, is commemorated in a magnificent stained glass window. A nineteenth-century diver who rescued the cathedral from sinking into the mire of the water meadows of the Itchen has a generous statue. Somewhat less peacefully, the rather gruesome death mask, of the last Catholic bishop – the fearsome Stephen Gardiner of Queen Mary's unhappy reign – is there for all to see. Worshippers and tourists normally flock in.

It was a beautiful June afternoon. The ancient cathedral seemed strangely still. The tourists were quiet and a small congregation prepared for an unusual event – unusual in the 1970s – a service of healing in an Anglican cathedral.

The speaker was a small, seemingly elderly man. He was in his sixties, but the ravages of war-time imprisonment by the Japanese made him look older. His high-pitched voice was quite difficult to hear. After the normal pleasantries, he launched into his talk with a personal reminiscence. Before the Second World War, Ken McAll[3] and his wife Frances had been missionaries in China. It was a threatening time, with constant danger both from the Red Army which was trying to wrest control from the Nationalistic government, and from the Japanese who were also invading parts of China. Ken, Eric Liddell[4] and other mission workers were increasingly aware of God's direction, and protection.

Ken explained that one day, he was returning to Siaochang along the rough road through the fields and heading towards the village, when he was aware of someone walking behind him. He was told not to go to that village, but to go instead to a different village, where he was needed. Ken took it to be the voice of a local farmer who knew what was going on. It was best not to show any fear by looking round.

When he reached the village, the gate was opened, and he was pulled inside. The villagers asked him what had made him change direction (some of them had watched him from afar). Ken said, 'That man out there told me to come,' but when he, and the locals, looked out there was no one else to be seen. Then Ken realized that his unseen companion had spoken in English – unlikely for a Chinese farmer!

The villagers then told him that if he had continued in the direction that he was heading, he would have landed in a Japanese trap, as the village to which he had been walking was occupied by Japanese troops. Moreover, a local skirmish had left several wounded, some of whom had been brought into the village, and several people needed his medical attention. One of the wounded became a Christian, and eventually joined the staff of the teacher training college where Eric Liddell had taught.

Ken knew that his life had been saved by the direct

intervention of the Lord. His world-view had changed. Writing about the incident[5], he commented,

> My mocking intolerance of the implicit belief of the Chinese in ghosts and the spirit world was gone. I understood, too, that the spirit world holds both good and evil influences, and I realised that my daily prayer for protection had been dramatically answered.

This was the highly unusual beginning to a very challenging talk. Ken continued with an account of his war-time captivity, shared with his wife, during which they had discovered that the power of prayer could replace unavailable medicines. As prisoners, they had been crammed into a freezing cold factory, into which some 1,200 prisoners had been herded by the Japanese.

The talk then moved on to tell of his more recent experiences of healing, including new insights into psychiatry which he had gained during post-war studies. He spoke as though the sort of experiences that he was relating should be part of our normal Christian life.

I listened spellbound. I had attended the meeting reluctantly (and how often are the most important meetings and services the ones to which we go with the greatest reluctance?). I should have been umpiring on the nearby school cricket field, or driving my car to help a natural history expedition. Instead, at the bidding of a saintly colleague, who had a seemingly eccentric interest in places and people of healing, I had persuaded Jane, my newly-wed wife, to join me in the cathedral.

Eventually the speaker was done. A time of prayer for healing followed including the laying-on of hands. My colleague, Philip, invited me to join him in the sanctuary. It would be nice to record that I witnessed instant answers to our prayers – I am not aware that we did, but I do know that I left the cathedral with a rather different world-view. For almost the first time in my life, I had met someone who had experienced the living Lord not only through conversion, prayer and worship; but also in power, in his presence and in miracles!

For me, an inexperienced young priest, listening to Ken McAll was another turning point. That afternoon, in Winchester Cathedral, was the first time I had ever heard someone speak directly about angels and healing. After a period of personal difficulties during which I had started to question some of the miraculous parts of the Bible, it was a great relief to hear first-hand evidence of the power of God.

A living testimony seemed worth a hundred books! I left the cathedral determined to find out more and with much greater expectation of what God was about to do in my life.

Concluding thoughts

We live, spiritually, in a strangely complacent age. All around us terrible things are happening – war, terrorism, drought, flooding and famine, HIV, global warming – the list is seemingly endless. Yet we are seldom shocked. Our post-modern age gazes at a pot-pourri of religious experiences with eyes full of gentle mockery. We do not want to be disturbed from our spiritual slumber. Like the citizens of ancient Athens, we enjoy talking about, and listening to, the latest ideas (Acts 17:21). We dislike any religious pathway that seems to point to a single truth. We, too, much prefer to believe in 'an unknown God'.

Stories about angels, and supernatural encounters, are of passing interest (useful to enliven dinner parties, casual conversations, Christmas sermons and evangelistic conversations). But to most people they are of no more significance than the sighting of a rare bird, an unusual orchid, or even the misfortunes of some well-known family.

In the Bible, and I believe in present-day experience, angels come unexpectedly both to stir people into action and to bring a much needed sense of awe and reverence into worship and daily living.

Perhaps my mind is too mathematical, but to me, if one of these stories, flawed jewels though they may be, truly testifies to an experience of the living God, then how much more does the witness of the Bible truly point us to Jesus – the central diamond in the universe?

If I can believe that Mark's angel (see p. 30) truly came to him in Norwich Cathedral Close, or Yun's account of his two prison escapes, or any other of these stories, then I can more easily believe that Mary's angel came to her in Nazareth (see Luke 1:26–38) and the various accounts of the angels at the empty tomb on the first Easter morning (John 20:10–18 for instance).

It seems very strange that myriads of people can believe in, and apparently experience, angelic help, and yet not take seriously the amazing events of the first Easter Day. Angels of today should point us back to angels at Bethlehem and beside the empty tomb, which in turn should lead us to want to seek, worship and follow Jesus.

We conclude this chapter with a visionary experience of one of Jesus' closest followers – John:

I turned around to see the voice that was speaking to me. And when I turned I saw seven golden lampstands, and among the lampstands was someone 'like a son of man', dressed in a robe reaching down to his feet and with a golden sash around his chest. His head and hair were white like wool, as white as snow, and his eyes were like blazing fire. His feet were like bronze glowing in a furnace, and his voice was like the sound of rushing waters. In his right hand he held seven stars, and out of his mouth came a sharp double-edged sword. His face was like the sun shining in all its brilliance. (Revelation 1:12–16)

The early church was about to enter a period of extreme persecution. John's experience must have been a tremendous reassurance for his personal faith, and an inspiration to his readers at a time when it must have seemed that the church could be swept away with its task scarcely begun.

Notes

1. Brother Yun, *The Heavenly Man*, Oxford: Monarch, 2002, from Chapters 6 and 22.
2. John Paton, *Missionary to the New Hebrides*, London: Hodder & Stoughton, 1893.
3. Frances and Kenneth McAll, *The Moon Looks Down*, Darley Anderson, 1987.
4. Eric Liddell, the famous missionary and Olympic gold medallist, died in captivity a few years later.
5. Dr Kenneth McAll, *Healing of the Family Tree*, London: SPCK, 1982 is his classic book.

CHAPTER 4

Angels Bring Help

IN THE LAST CHAPTER, we saw how angels protect some of God's servants in times of extreme danger. In this chapter, we look at some other examples of angelic help and note how angels seem to be particularly *visible* to children.

Carol Vorderman investigates

Ray and Pam Fardon, who once helped me with a Parish Mission, told me a wonderful story of protection, and escape from disaster. In the late 1960s, they were leading a youth camp at Lee Abbey, near Lynton, in North Devon. Pam was enjoying the beauty of the coastline, when suddenly her thoughts were disturbed by the loud noise of an engine.

She looked up and saw a tractor, out of control, careering wildly down a steep field. The driver managed to steer it through a gate, but it was gaining speed all the time as it raced through a second field. By now, many of the guests at the house on the top of the hill, and many in the youth camp, were watching with horror. They started to pray for the tractor driver who was trying desperately to bring his machine under control. The tractor was racing towards a car park crowded with holidaymakers, eating their picnics. Pam remembers praying, 'Lord, please change its direction.' Moments later, it veered aside, missed the car park, and somersaulted over the cliff.

Ray took a few men with him and raced down the cliff pathway, instructing everyone else to pray. Quickly, Ray found the tractor upside down on a car parked by a chalet on the beach, far below the original scene. The owner, a widowed mother of a large family, had just left the car and wandered back to the chalet, wondering why she had got out of the car. Her car was completely crushed, but no one was hurt.

Ray, and his friends, searched for the tractor driver, but there was no sign of anyone. A little while later, the original tractor driver, who had got out of the tractor leaving the engine running while he opened a gate, appeared on the scene. Pam and Ray and others were certain they had seen someone driving the tractor, and steering so that it avoided the car park. Pam, at the time, described a man in brown, leaning right over the steering wheel with his hands almost crossed over.

Ray, Pam and others who witnessed the scene, are quite convinced that they saw an angel driving the tractor. Like many similar other stories, it is simpler to believe that the second driver was an angel. The alternative is that a number of people all suffered hallucinations; and that, by chance, the tractor swerved to avoid ploughing into the car park.

Lee Abbey is a great place of prayer, a place where others have seen angels and heard them singing. Its founder, Jack Winslow[1] wrote a book which includes many stories of miraculous protection, and several about angels. Many stories about angels are stories of protection, usually from extreme danger from people hostile to the Christian gospel.

Carol Vorderman included this story in a TV investigation that she did on the paranormal. The 'expert' view seemed to be that the watchers 'saw' the tractor driver driving the vehicle because that is what they would expect to see. That rational view fails to explain the extraordinary way in which the tractor was manoeuvred to avoid driving through the crowded campsite.

My editor asks, rather more pertinently, why didn't the angel stop the engine or put the brake on? It would seem that angels seem concerned with saving life and not property. If the angel had stopped the tractor there would have been no story! God seems to allow these incidents to give us glimpses of his sovereign power.

God protects evangelists

Another example of God's protection comes from Albania. In the 1950s, Albania was declared to be world's first official atheistic state. The Christians were vilified, and persecuted. Outside, some intercessors felt called to prayer. A few intrepid tourists carried Bibles into this dangerous country, and tried to make contact with Christians.

Then communism collapsed, and the country began to open up. About the same time, in 1990, a Somerset businessman, Ian Loring, was facing a personal crisis. An unpleasant business career had come to a dramatic end, and he had been fired. At the age of twenty-seven, he was unemployed, and not particularly employable. In a Bristol shopping centre, he saw and heard a typical open-air gospel presentation. He was singularly unmoved, impressed neither by the clever reverse lettering used by the evangelist Korki Davey, nor by the testimony of a converted Irishman 'from the mire to the choir'.

About two months later, reflecting on an increasingly

uncertain future, and relaxing in the bath, he was startled to hear a quiet authoritative voice: 'Do not store up for [yourself] treasures on earth, where moth and rust destroy... But store up for [yourself] treasures in heaven... For where your treasure is, there your heart will be also. No one can serve two masters. Either he will hate the one and love the other, or he will be devoted to the one, and despise the other. You cannot serve both God and Money.' (See Matthew 6:19–21,24.)

Ian knew that, for whatever reason, God had chosen to speak to him. In early 1991, after some training in evangelism, he found himself travelling towards Albania. The group's first attempts at evangelism took place in a railway siding in Northern Greece, where they found, and fed, a group of hungry Albanian refugees. They gave the group some copies of Luke's Gospel.

The next night they returned with more food; but the refugees had been fed in quite a different way. Their leader said, in Albanian, 'Last night, I read your book to the men. I told them that it was important for them to listen. In the morning when I awoke, they were looking at me. No one was saying anything! Their faces were different. I said to them, "You all saw him too, didn't you?"' He continued, 'Last night, he stood there by the fire. His clothes were white and clean. He said to us, "You are my sheep, and I am your shepherd. Come to me", and he held out his hands.'

This was an extraordinary encouragement to Ian and his team. Often the work was hard, and very dangerous; occasionally there were other conversions through the direct intervention of God. On one occasion, he needed a different sort of help. Crossing from Albania into Northern Greece could be hazardous, as the Greeks weren't too keen either on Protestant evangelists, or their evangelical literature. He writes:

Caralee and I felt deeply in need of a rest in Thessaloniki. I had been leading a huge number of Bible studies, and the constant stream of visitors from the growing church fellowship to our room in Little Paris, sometimes from 8 a.m. through to 11 p.m. was draining. So was the feeling of living in a fishbowl, being constantly watched by others: along with Mike Brown, we were the only foreigners living in the market town for the region's 250,000 people. Sometimes, when we reached Greece, we would sleep for 24 hours at a stretch to recover.

On this day, when we reached the Greek side of the border, we discovered their customs officers were on strike. I asked a policeman if it was still okay to pass through, and he told me it was fine by him. However, as Caralee began to drive past the customs point, a man in a light grey uniform jumped up on to the footplate, yanked open my door and dragged me down on to the road. As my side hit the ground, he was going berserk, shouting, punching me in the stomach and kicking me in the back and kidneys. I was completely stunned by the assault. Other customs officers were gathering around, and I could hear Caralee screaming at them.

When the beating had finished, my sides were raw and I felt sick and in shock. We were made to park up our vehicle and led away towards a police Land Rover. We had driven through the customs officers' picket line, and the man, a stocky colonel with a high forehead, was shouting that he was going to have us arrested.

'You have tried to enter our country with violence,' he raged, scarlet-faced. I couldn't believe the accusation. We were driven away from the border point with the colonel and a police officer sitting stiffly in the front. I looked at Caralee: she had tears in her eyes.

Two of my ribs were too sensitive to touch, and I didn't know what was going to happen to us. The officer was offering no explanations, and the colonel kept repeating his charge.

After a short drive the car drew into the Greek town of Kastoria and pulled up outside the courthouse. The colonel marched us roughly inside the building. We sat there waiting for an unbearably long time in a plain room with a single wooden bench. I felt deeply upset and afraid: we were in a foreign country, unable to speak the language and facing a trumped-up charge. Caralee's hand felt warm as I held it, and we prayed together furiously.

The colonel entered shortly and presented us with a document and a black Biro. 'Sign this... here,' he shouted gruffly. It was written in Greek, which neither of us could read, but I assumed it was some admission of our offence. Another policeman was attempting to translate but saying little more than, 'Sign here, please.'

As I pushed the document away, my hand was shaking. 'Look,' I said angrily, 'we'd like to speak to a lawyer.'

'You haven't got a lawyer,' the colonel snapped sarcastically. 'You're in Greece now. You'll sign it, or else you'll be forgotten about!' It was an ominous statement.

At that very moment, a tall, olive-skinned man in a blue pin-striped suit entered the room. Under his arm he held a buffed briefcase and an Oxford legal dictionary. 'I'll be your lawyer,' he announced in an upper-class English accent.

No one said a word: everyone was equally stunned. The man spoke quickly in Greek, and the colonel and the officer left the room. He sat down next to Caralee without introducing himself. 'Tell me what has happened,' he said, and I explained the events of the last couple of hours with a huge sense of relief.

'Wait here,' he replied, 'I shan't be long.'

Half an hour later we entered the courtroom with the man now representing us. 'Sit there with me,' he said, 'You will be all right. Just say that you are sorry when I tell you.'

There were three judges presiding over the session that day in Kastoria courthouse: two men, and a woman sitting in the middle, all of them dressed in black and red legal robes. The policeman spoke first, then the customs colonel, and then our lawyer. The colonel spoke again with a red face, raising his voice angrily. Our lawyer spoke once more, and then the room went silent.

Neither Caralee nor I could understand a word of what was being said.

As I waited, I felt tense and cold. I shuffled uncomfortably in the chair and cast my eyes around the room. Directly behind the woman judge was a large Orthodox painting of the resurrected Christ with his arms outstretched towards us. Across the courtroom roof, the painting fanned out to depict a grey-bearded God the Father looking down from a patch of blue sky between the clouds. I studied the painting for a long minute. A strong sensation came over me that in this room Jesus was going to be both our judge and our advocate, and my spirits began to lift.

The woman judge stood up and slammed her hammer down on the bench. She turned towards us and announced: 'You are without blame, and free to go. I'm sorry.' The sense of relief and vindication was phenomenal. She then turned to the colonel and began to berate him at length. He seemed to shrink a little before her and turned even redder in the face.

Outside the courtroom, we shook our lawyer's hand firmly. 'Could we have your card? We still don't know your name,' I enquired. 'What do we owe you?'

'Oh, it's all right,' the man replied, already stepping away. 'You would have done the same for me.' Then he was gone through the front door of the courthouse.

I looked at Caralee and she at me. It was a little strange. The police officer escorted us back to the car, and the colonel sat without speaking in the front. As we drove towards the border, he reached back and offered his hand. I shook it, lightly at first, but then with firmness as he looked at me with his pride now diminished.

The whole incident left a deep impression on us. It seemed to underline in our hearts God's amazing care, even if we strayed over the edge – in this instance through a picket line. And as for our free lawyer who had so quickly disappeared, who was he? An angel with an Oxford legal dictionary?

The next time we arrived at the border, the colonel greeted me like an old friend, hugging me warmly and offering me a glass of ouzo. It was as if, like children, we'd had a fight and made up and now he respected me. Whenever I needed help getting people or goods through the border from then on, it was the colonel's pleasure to make the process smooth.[2]

It seems to me, that it is far more likely that Ian's lawyer was an angel than an actual English-speaking lawyer who turned up at the right time, with the necessary diplomatic skills to rescue two very frightened evangelists in a remote part of Greece.

This story fits the category of angels who appear as human beings. Only afterwards did the recipients of their help realize the true nature of their helpers. In the earlier story, there is no doubt that the Albanians were visited by the Lord, dressed in brilliant white, as they studied Luke's Gospel.

Angels as unexpected helpers

As I have researched for this book, I have been surprised and encouraged by meeting many people who seem to have had first-hand encounters with angels.

Don Latham, an old friend, told me how, some years ago, he was just leaving the M32 in Bristol to drive up the M4 to catch a plane at Heathrow Airport. He had allowed a reasonable amount of time, but just as he was changing motorways his smart, well-serviced car stuttered to a halt. He got out and opened the bonnet. Nothing was obviously wrong and he started to pray.

He was about to travel overseas on a major speaking trip, and the inconvenience to many other people if he missed the plane would have been considerable. Almost immediately someone appeared and asked if he could help. For a short time the unknown helper fiddled around under the bonnet. He then turned to Don and told him that the car would get him to the airport, but that he'd better get it seen to as soon as he returned.

On his return, Don took the car straight to his normal

garage. When they had looked at it, they expressed some amazement that he'd been able to drive it anywhere.

There are many similar stories in the literature about angels; one of the most dramatic inspired the book *Where Angels Walk*[3]. The author's son, Tim, was trapped on Christmas Eve 1983, in sub-zero temperatures on a lonely highway on the coldest night in American Mid-West records. Tim, and a friend, had been driving home to see their family in Chicago. Unfortunately, the car had crawled to a frozen halt. To leave the car was to invite certain death on such a night, to wait and hope for rescue wasn't a much brighter option. They prayed, and drifted off, as if into a dream, in the cold. They were woken, not by the lights of an oncoming vehicle, but by a knock on the window and an offer of help. Their rescuer, who said nothing else, was driving a tow truck. He towed them back to where, earlier in the evening they had dropped off a friend, and where if they'd had any sense they would have asked to stay the night. When they arrived, Tim raced into his friend's house to ask to borrow money to pay for the tow. His friend commented, 'I don't see any tow truck out there.' Not only was there no sign of a truck, but there was only one set of tyre marks in the snow – and they belonged to Tim's car!

Angels bring comfort

Several of my parishioners, past and present, have related experiences which point to angelic help. Here is one example:

Marjorie told me about her first husband's death. She was quite young, and the day of the funeral had been exhausting and emotional. In the afternoon while the funeral gathering was taking place in her house, she was struck down by a terrible migraine. Exhausted and shaken, she retired to bed.

Quite suddenly in the corner of her bedroom, she saw a wonderfully bright light; she felt that angels were present, and she remembered one of her favourite hymns (*Immortal Invisible* God only wise, in light inaccessible hid from our eyes), whose last verse runs as follows:

> Great Father of glory, pure Father of Light,
> Thine angels adore Thee, all veiling their sight;
> All laud we would render; O help us to see
> 'Tis only the splendour of light hideth Thee.
>
> *Walter Chalmers Smith*

Years later, on Pentecost Sunday 1994, we had a particularly powerful time of worship. After the sermon, the preacher prayed for the Holy Spirit to touch people – inviting them to stand, kneel, or sit, as they felt appropriate. Marjorie, sitting in the choir stalls, had an overwhelming sense of God's presence; and again she was aware of being enveloped in bright light. She found this very moving at the time; and very comforting, especially at times of serious illness, in subsequent years.

Angels and children

Over the centuries, theologians have argued about the extent that guardian angels are available to protect people. Thomas Aquinas (c. 1225–74) wrote a huge treatise on the subject. But at the end of his life, after a mystical experience of Christ's presence, he said that this was worth far more than all his writings.

Experience suggests, and this seems to accord with Jesus' teaching, that children are particularly aware of angels. Here are several examples:

We have always enjoyed stories about angels in the family and have prayed for their protection on many occasions. When my eldest daughter, aged about four at the time, was experiencing fears associated with the dark and worrying about what was behind the door of a long wardrobe in her bedroom, we prayed together about it.

One day shortly after, she remarked to me that she had dreamt there was a shining lady at the end of the wardrobe and that she was no longer afraid – only she wished that the lady could be there all the time. A year or so later when she had started school she was persistently asking me about how one could see an angel and, more particularly, if she could see an angel. I told her that God would send angels as messengers when he needed to. I told her to pray that night that he would send an angel to her one day too. The next morning, she awoke with an account of a vivid dream of angels, in the playground at school with children gathered round. We used this image to help her through all manner of playground and school problems that cropped up in the early years.

The moments remain in our memories very clearly, in the same way that other times when the Lord has spoken to me very directly have too. A sort of gift of an imprint to remain for future reassurance and comfort.

Looking back on her short life to date, I realise that the Lord has blessed her so richly with signs and gifts and now, at almost thirteen, she has a profound faith that shines out to those closely associated with her. In her gentle way she has been instrumental in bringing several of her friends to a deeper understanding of Jesus, and this has come about in the simplest of ways – a question, friendship, generosity, concern and probably many others of the ways she sets me an example of being Christlike!

Emma's angels

Just before the new millennium began, Don Latham, a well-known author and speaker, led a Parish Weekend for us. His powerful theme 'See that you fulfil your potential' (see Colossians 4:17) left many of us very challenged. It confirmed to me that I should seek a change of direction for the last few years of my active ministry. He, also, spoke of angels and protection (see above).

One of our parishioners, Clare, had never really thought about this aspect of Christianity. Angels were in the pages of the Bible, not in today's church. Soon afterwards, an incident during a family holiday in Majorca changed her mind. Here is her story:

We had just arrived in Majorca, and had decided to take the children straight down to the beach. Hannah (seven), Tim (five) and Emma (three) were making sandcastles and we were sitting close by watching and talking. We suddenly realised that we could not see Emma. The others had been so absorbed in making their castle that they hadn't noticed her go.

We started rushing along the beach looking for her, not leaving Hannah and Tim out of our sight. I described her to lots of people in case they had seen her. The beach was very crowded and Emma was very small, and she didn't seem to be anywhere. The sea was in front of us, a busy road behind, and a yachting marina about half a mile away, so there were lots of dangers. I panicked and called the police and then waited and prayed with Hannah and Tim while Simon continued to search up and down the beach.

I prayed so hard and so intensely for Emma to be returned to us safely. I knew the only thing I could do was to put the situation in God's hands. Suddenly, a man ran up to me (at this point Emma had been missing for nearly forty minutes) and told me that his wife had Emma and was carrying her back to us along the beach.

I ran with him towards his wife, and Emma was safely in her arms. We all cried, and Emma was very relieved to be back with us.

The couple were very fair and somehow glowed with an inner light which made them seem radiant. They shook our hands and we thanked them again and again, and then they left. When we turned round to look for them they had disappeared.

Emma has always told us that the angels came and found her and brought her back to us. She had reached the marina when they found her and picked her up – at the very point when she was in most danger.

We know that God sent his angels to protect her and bring her back safely to us.

God's protection for a family and guardian angels for a child

In 2005, Jane and I visited Papua New Guinea. Jane was able to revisit Dogura where she had taught in 1971, and I was speaking to the large gathering of Wycliffe Bible translators at their centre in Ukarumpa. Amongst many testimonies of God's protection and provision of guardian angels, we received this from Anita Synnott:

My name is Anita, my husband is Sean and we have two children of our own, Lachlan (five years old) and Courtney (four years old). We live in Ukarumpa in the Eastern Highlands of Papua New Guinea. Our job here is to provide a home for the children of Missionaries who are working in this country. We currently have six children boarding with us. We have been up here for four years and we pray everyday for our safety and for angels to surround us. God has been so faithful!

In July 2004, we were to attend a church retreat and Sean was going to drive to the next town (Goroka) to get a flight. Lachlan, Courtney and I, were flying out from Ukarumpa. We had only found out the day before that there was no room on the flight for Sean. So, that morning, Sean and I prayed together for his safety and off he went. He was driving along about thirty-five minutes from home, when a gang of armed 'rascals' confronted him. Sean stopped the car and the rascals moved Sean into the back of the twelve-seater bus. They started driving and asking him for money and started going through his backpack and pockets of his shorts.

About ten minutes later the bus suddenly stopped and

the rascals started to flee. Sean also got out of the bus and then heard gunfire. As he looked up, he saw a police block and they were firing at the bus and the rascals who were running away behind him. Sean stood there with his arms raised as the bullets miraculously flew between him, the car and the rascals.

Eventually the police were close enough for Sean to explain to them what had happened. It is a miracle that Sean wasn't shot, all too often, the police here shoot first then ask questions.

In September 2004, Courtney and I needed to go to Lae (a town on the coast) to join Sean and Lachlan who were there already. We were travelling down with friends in a twelve-seater van. Before we left, we prayed for angels to surround us and we put our lives in God's hands.

About twenty-five minutes into the trip, we were about to cross a single-lane bridge when our left-hand tyre hit the left-hand side of the bridge. For a few seconds, we were on the side of the bridge balancing on our axle. I remember thinking, 'How are we going to lift the bus off the edge of this bridge?' The next thing I remember, there was a lot of noise and everything was dark. We had tumbled off the bridge, seven metres into the river below landing on the side of the bus.

When we stopped moving, I realised that I wasn't dead, then realised that I was under the water. I was able to push a few people off of me and then get some air. I wasn't sure how deep the water was, but knew that we had to get out of the bus quickly. There were five children, and five adults on board. At the time of the crash,

Courtney wasn't sitting with me and there are no seat belts fitted in the back of these buses.

When I was sure that I wasn't dead (it sounds silly now, but it seemed to make sense at the time!) I realised that I had to find little Courtney. She was wearing a brightly coloured dress and I could see it in the water about a metre from where I was. I was able to reach into the water and pick her up. By this time, there were some people outside the bus to help us. So I passed Courtney out and then we all followed. We all walked away from the accident!

Late that day, I was talking to Courtney about the 'big bump' and was reassuring her and trying to make her understand that it was God who protected us. I told her that God is everywhere and will always look after us. After thinking this over for a few seconds, she piped up with the comment that she didn't see God there. I was wondering how I was to explain this to a child, when she said, 'I didn't see God, I just saw the angels.'

As tears filled my eyes (and still do every time I think of it!) I asked her what she meant. *'The angels were there and when the bump came, they hugged me.'* She said that they were warm and fluffy and all of the colours of the rainbow. I was full of questions and was overwhelmed with the image of my God protecting my child with his angels. I was sure that I was going to die and I even recall thinking of the movie *Titanic*... just get to the top of the ship/bus! Meanwhile Courtney told me of the angels singing to her; she asked what my angels sang to me!

There are so many details that God worked out for us! The way that we were all sitting, the seat belt that was repaired for the driver just the day before and that no luggage was on top of Courtney! The river was only about a metre deep, any deeper and we would have been in trouble and any less, and the impact of landing could have been devastating. Instead, we all walked away with only a few minor injuries.

I am sure that there are many incidents in which God has interceded on our behalf, ones that I am not even aware of. I know that God answers our prayers and he doesn't allow us to endure more than we can handle. He is sovereign and what an awesome thing it is to have a God who knows us all so intimately!

These three stories came from former parishioners and a missionary in Papua New Guinea; here is one from a new friend. A lady, from a different faith, who has had a very tragic life, shared a story about her son.

When he was eight, he fell into a canal. He couldn't swim, and he cried out to God for help. He saw a bright light, and then felt himself pulled out of the water by a man, who promptly disappeared. He walked home dripping wet, and some while later told me the story of his remarkable rescue.

Christ's light and love seem to be touching this family, but the story of her son's rescue suggests that guardian angels do not confine themselves to Christians.

Angels and animals

A missionary in Papua New Guinea told me how one evening his children woke up screaming. He was translating the New Testament in a difficult area where there was a lot of spiritual activity. He commanded whatever had entered their hut to leave in the name of Jesus. He was aware of a presence departing. Moments later, he heard a commotion amongst the animals of the village. This was followed by children crying. A few minutes later, down the valley in another village there was a repetition – first the animals and then the children cried.

This was one of a number of such experiences that this family endured. The missionary then commented to me 'I couldn't tell this story in my home country.' 'Why?' I asked. 'Because no one would believe me – and they would probably stop funding me,' he replied sadly.

What a devastating reflection on the rationalistic views of the church in the West!

June Jolly's testimony

June Jolly was a Nursing Officer at the Brook Hospital, Woolwich, in SE London. In 1973 she won a scholarship from the Florence Nightingale Fellowship and the Rayne Foundation to study family involvement with sick children in a thirteen-week visit to Canada, the United States and Jamaica. The object was to establish what could make the hospitalization of children more friendly and comfortable for them and their families, such as open visiting, and to find out what other countries did.

One of the many places she visited was Vancouver, BC. One morning, she was walking through a suburb of the city in order to get to the hospital she was studying. As she did not have to be there until ten o'clock most people had already gone to work and the streets were deserted. Typically, the houses had no fences or gates so she was not surprised when an Alsatian dog came bounding towards her.

She likes animals, and her first reaction was to think 'nice dog', but as it got nearer it curled its lip, and bared its teeth and growled. Her immediate reaction was to throw her arms across her body and to say very rapidly, 'Lord Jesus, protect me by your angels!'

By then the dog was on its hind legs, still snarling and baring its teeth, but clawing with its front paws at something invisible about a foot in front of her. She felt as if she had had a perspex tube placed around her, although the dog's scratching made no sound. It simply could get no nearer.

She was not at all frightened – having asked for protection she knew she was receiving it. She was so confident of this that when she wondered whether she was protected at the back as well as the front she turned around while the animal carried on growling and clawing in the same position. She then decided that the situation was ridiculous and walked on, whereupon the dog simply trotted off. She has no idea why she mentioned angels.

There was a sequel to this. During the late 1970s, June experienced a lot of trouble in communicating properly with her sister. She would get very worked up and would not be able to say what she wanted in the way she wanted, and even if she did then her words were misconstrued. Then one day the Lord reminded her that as he had protected her physically from the dog, so he could protect her emotionally. The next time she spoke to her sister she prayed for protection and has had no trouble since. While she used to pray after the first time, she finds she no longer needs to now.

June's comment on this is 'if the devil finds that he can't get in, he will eventually trot off like the dog'.

This is one of a number of stories that I have heard about the sensitivity of animals to unseen presences. A doctor and his wife told me how their first marital home, in a Somerset village, was haunted. They were fairly calm about the strange things that they saw and experienced. By contrast, their dog was absolutely miserable and often refused to go up the stairs. Personally, I regard the evidence of animals as very persuasive. Many animals, especially dogs, seem sensitive to any untoward spiritual presences in buildings and even in people.

Summary

This chapter illustrates how God uses angels to protect people. In some cases, we may prefer a *rational* explanation – the Greek lawyer was a real person, the tractor missed the campsite by providence, the children just thought they saw angels... Even if there was a *rational* explanation in *some* of the cases, the overall sense of God's protection and provision is undeniable. The question, which is unanswerable, is why were these people so privileged?

The same dilemma faced the early church. The apostle James (Acts 12:1–2) was executed by Herod; Peter escaped. James was one of the inner three whom Jesus especially trained for the work of spreading the good news of the kingdom. He didn't live long enough to achieve anything of lasting significance. Missionaries have answered God's call and been killed or died of disease almost as soon as they have arrived. Missionaries in Zimbabwe have had miraculous escapes, but many of their colleagues have been killed. The Tsunami on 26 December 2004 shook the world and raised all these questions even more acutely. Some people had miraculous escapes, many did not.

Theological questions considered

There are a number of theological points that need to be made. First: Jesus warned his hearers about the possibility of accidents (see Luke 13:1–5). He said in effect that accidents are part of our fallen world and that people who are killed in this way are no different from anyone else, but that accidents are a warning to all of us to repent and be living in a right relationship with God.

Secondly: Jesus taught that there would be an increase in natural disasters as the world drew to its close 'There will be signs in the sun, moon and stars. On the earth, nations will be in anguish and perplexity at *the roaring and tossing of the sea*' (Luke 21:25, my italics).

Thirdly, and most importantly, Paul recognized that the created order had become imperfect when he wrote about creation groaning and waiting for freedom (see Romans 8:18–22).

Fourthly, Jesus constantly warned his followers to expect persecution. For instance he said 'a time is coming when anyone who kills you will think he is offering a service to God' (John 16:2).

We cannot know the reasons why God permits these things to happen; what we can know is that the rescues and other interventions that we have been thinking about did not happen by some fluke; they happened as part of God's sovereign plan. We have a choice – we can respond in faith believing in God's providential protection *and accept that accidents, persecutions and tragedies are also part of the world in which we live.* The alternatives are unbelief or a form of Deism which denies the possibility of God's intervention.

After the Tsunami which devastated so many people lives on Boxing Day 2004, the correspondence columns of national newspapers were understandably filled with letters making challenges to any form of belief in a supernatural power. Yet even the horrors of the Tsunami yielded many strange stories of preservation as well as much heart-rending tragedy. An understanding of the teachings of Jesus and the Bible on these matters is increasingly necessary as we face a world where natural disasters seem to be increasing year on year.[4]

Notes

1. Jack Winslow, *Modern Miracles*, London: Hodder & Stoughton, 1968, Chapter 5.
2. Muthena Alkazraji, *Christ and the Kalashnikov*, pp. 60ff., London: Marshall Pickering, 2001. Used by permission of Zondervan Inc. Many other stories of protection of evangelists can be found in Christian literature, often in situations of considerable danger.
3. Joan Anderson, *Where Angels Walk*, London: Hodder & Stoughton, 1992, Chapter 1.
4. The devastation caused in August 2005 by hurricane Katrina in and around New Orleans was just one more natural catastrophe.

CHAPTER 5

Angels and Conversion

THROUGHOUT CHRISTIAN HISTORY there have been a number of significant and unusually dramatic conversions. The most famous was that of Paul, who as Saul of Tarsus, had his famous vision of the risen Jesus on the Damascus road (see Acts 9:1–9). Angels were directly involved in two conversions recorded in the Acts of the Apostles. One of the most effective missionaries in the church was Philip. After a fruitful and controversial ministry in Samaria, Philip encountered an angel.

> Now an angel of the Lord said to Philip, 'Go south to the road – the desert road – that goes down from Jerusalem to Gaza.' So he started out, and on his way he met an Ethiopian eunuch, an important official in charge of all the treasury of Candace, queen of the Ethiopians. This man had gone to Jerusalem to worship, and on his way home was sitting in his chariot reading the book of Isaiah the prophet. The Spirit told Philip, 'Go to that chariot and stay near it.' (Acts 8:26–29)

The result of this encounter was the baptism, in the desert, and conversion of a highly influential Ethiopian from whom the Coptic Christians trace their spiritual descent. Soon afterwards the conversion of a leading Roman, again after an angelic intervention, took place.

At Caesarea there was a man named Cornelius, a centurion in what was known as the Italian Regiment. He and all his family were devout and God-fearing; he gave generously to those in need and prayed to God regularly. One day at about three in the afternoon he had a vision. He distinctly saw an angel of God, who came to him and said, 'Cornelius!'

Cornelius stared at him in fear. 'What is it, Lord?' he asked.

The angel answered, 'Your prayers and gifts to the poor have come up as a memorial offering before God. Now send men to Joppa to bring back a man named Simon who is called Peter. He is staying with Simon the tanner, whose house is by the sea.'

When the angel who spoke to him had gone, Cornelius called two of his servants and a devout soldier who was one of his attendants. He told them everything that had happened and sent them to Joppa. (Acts 10:1–8)

Peter, who needed far more persuading, had a curious vision (Acts 10:9–16) which makes no sense until the Holy Spirit tells him that, 'Three men are looking for you'! The first result of this dramatic encounter was that Peter invited his Gentile visitors to stay with him; the second was the clear conversion of a Gentile household. It is impossible to overemphasize what a barrier, both social and spiritual, had to be overcome; comparable perhaps, in modern times, to the problem of apartheid in South Africa.

There is a clear distinction between Cornelius' vision of an angel, and the Holy Spirit's work with Peter. At the end of the story, the Holy Spirit takes over (Acts 10:44–48), intervening to touch Cornelius and his household, even before Peter has finished preaching!

In the next few centuries, supernatural encounters were quite common. For instance, the well-documented conversion of Augustine in the fourth century made a huge difference to the church both at that time and in the future; while the conversion of King Edwin in the seventh century made a significant difference to the religious history of the British Isles. Visions and supernatural happenings were very significant in both stories[1], but we are going to concentrate on more recent examples.

Angels who show the way to God

The conversion of Sundar Singh

At the beginning of the twentieth century, Sundar Singh, the fifteen-year-old son of a wealthy Sikh landowner, was desperate. His mother had just died, and his own spiritual quest, which had included education at a good school run by missionaries and searching the holy writings of the Sikhs, the Hindus and the Muslims, had led him nowhere. He prayed to God to reveal himself to him. He had decided that if there was no answer, he would commit suicide by throwing himself in front of an express train, which would pass his home at 5 a.m. He woke at 3 a.m, took his early-morning bath, which Sikhs and Hindus always have before worship, and returned to pray. He expected one of the gods to speak to him.

What happened changed his life. He saw the radiant figure of Jesus, whose followers he had hated at school. He heard a voice saying, 'Why do you persecute me? I died on the cross for you and the whole world.' The cloud disappeared and he went to wake his father to tell him what had happened. His family was furious, eventually sending him out of the family home with poisoned food.

Sundar became a most respected Christian evangelist, he travelled the world, had the joy of seeing his father converted and had a number of experiences, during his evangelistic ministry, of angels.[2] This story illustrates the ways in which God can call and protect his servants. We cannot presume on this, and Sundar himself disappeared when crossing the mountains on his way to another evangelistic mission in Tibet.

The angel and the Eskimo leader

About the same time, something remarkable was happening in north east Canada, on the edge of Baffin Island where the seer of the local Eskimos, a man called Angutirjuaq, had heard about a god, whom he knew as Jesusi. After a great dream of light and darkness, he started a spiritual search to see if Jesusi was the way to the truth.

He followed a tribal custom and went to search for seal meat, on a dark moonless night. He decided that if he found a seal, made a kill and could share it with his followers, then he would follow the new way. Very quickly, despite the lack of moonlight, he found a hole where seals come up to breathe. In the bitter cold of the Arctic night, he managed to fall asleep.

When he awoke, he was astonished, because the ice-hole was lit up. He could even see a seal in the hole. Far more remarkably, he was aware of three bright figures in the sky. He harpooned the seal, made his way back to his camp, and told his followers of his decision to follow Jesusi.

Years later, Canon John Turner arrived as a missionary. Angutirjuaq's grandson was one of the first to respond to clearer teaching about the way of Jesus. But then things started to go badly wrong. As so often happens, contact with the missionaries was followed by greater contact with Canadian traders, and that opened up the way to liquor. The Eskimo communities became renowned for drunkenness, violence and sex.

By the early 1990s, the suicide rate, particularly amongst the teenagers, was rising dramatically. The few remaining Christians turned to prayer. Some of the effects of a dramatic ongoing revival can be seen on the Transformations II Video[3]. Apart from huge social changes, for the better, in schools, community, environment and churches, there were some supernatural signs – particularly an inexplicable deep sound heard, and caught on tape, at one of their revival meetings.

This strange phenomenon occurred as Looee Arreak, one of the youth leaders, started to pray for some of the young people. There was already a deep sense of repentance, and a desire to be cleansed based on the Beatitude 'Blessed are the pure in heart, for they will see God' (Matthew 5:8). The supernatural sound, like the sound of many voices, started softly, and then built up to a crescendo, causing everything and everyone to shake. The pastor thought that something had gone wrong with their sound switchboard. He turned it off completely and the sound continued; it was nothing to do with the human recording system. Amazingly, the tape recorder still recorded the sound – something completely impossible to explain.

There was, and is, a tremendous sense of awe and wonder. In many neighbouring communities, it was also obvious that God was bringing transformation. The angels who visited the old seer, Angutirjuaq, about a hundred years ago, seem to be guarding the community, and encouraging their people's new found faith.

Angels in Dartmoor

It would be hard to find a greater contrast to either Angutirjuaq or Sundar than Fred Lemon. I heard Fred give his testimony in Oxford Town Hall. It was at a healing meeting led by my old friend Fred Smith. Fred Smith[4] was no stranger to miracles – even that night a man walked in yellow with cancer, walked out looking very well, and when I contacted him some months later said that he had been completely healed; but it was Fred Lemon who had the strangest story. It ran something like this:

In my younger days, I was a serious criminal. One day, with some others, I robbed a jeweller's shop in London. Unfortunately, there was some violence; we left the jeweller almost dead. Soon afterwards, we were arrested and brought to trial. The jeweller's life hung in the balance, so did mine. If he had died, according to the law at the time, we would have certainly been hung.

Fortunately, he recovered, I was given a long stretch, and ended up in Dartmoor. It was a gloomy terrible place, and I made little attempt to socialise or to get educated. I was one of the most hopeless cases, among a group of desperate lost people. Then on 10th August 1950, I awoke to find three men standing in front of me in my cell. It was in the middle of the night, but the dark gloomy cell was flooded with light.

The angel on the right, said 'Fred, this is Jesus,' pointing to the figure in the middle. I was aware of the presence of Jesus. He started to tell me all about my past life.

Strangely, I didn't feel afraid. He told me how he had died to pay the penalty for my sins, and through his resurrection that he had overcome the power of death.

Significantly, at the end of a wonderful speech, he said, 'If you want to become a Christian, you must drive the hatred from your heart.' I knew that he was speaking the truth. I was well aware that I had an extreme hatred, especially towards some of the prison warders, and that I had even contemplated attempting to murder some of them. I had been listening with my head in my hands, but with this last sentence I looked up; the three men still looking at me were fading through the wall. There was a distinct click, and I was alone. I knew that Jesus and two of his angels had chosen to visit me. I wasn't afraid. In fact, immediately, I lay down and fell into a deep and peaceful sleep.

Fred went on to tell how his life had been instantly transformed by God's grace. It hadn't been easy, in many ways people found the new Fred more difficult to understand than the old one. Years later, after his release, Fred Lemon wrote a book[5], and liked nothing better than to travel around giving his testimony to God's grace, and telling of the unexpected visitors in his prison cell.

Angel choirs in hospital

On 10 March 2002, I was preaching in Holy Trinity, Leicester. It was my first Sunday on the staff of this large church. The vicar invited people to come forward for prayer. Rosemary Carr, who was visiting one of her family, came up. A few days later, she wrote to me with this story:

I was in hospital for an operation in September 1995 and the following occurred in the early hours of the Sunday I was there. There were just three of us in the ward over the weekend – an elderly lady dying of cancer next to me, and one other, also post operative, opposite us. The poor lady next to me was continually crying out in pain and fear, so I went to her and offered to pray with her for restful sleep, which she gladly accepted. As I struggled back to bed, I was assailed by nasty gargoyle-like faces, and knew it to be the enemy's retaliation. I cried out to Jesus to send his angelic protection.

Almost immediately I heard distant music, which I assumed was a radio, but as it came nearer and louder, I realized it was an angelic choir – such high and beautiful notes in strangely familiar music – and soon, through the central aisle of the ward came a procession of angels, so tall and ethereally glorious, playing old-fashioned instruments like the lutes, etc. one sees on Christmas cards. I don't know how long this went on, but I was transfixed with wonder and praise.

And then I was aware of Jesus amongst them. (I did not see his face, but his presence was tangible in the spirit sense.) He had not come for my dying neighbour as I thought, but went across to the other patient. She was a hospital sister from the A and E Ward. Two of her three teenage children were special needs children. I saw in the Spirit her family all around her bed, and Jesus came and embraced them each, one by one, and then collectively as a family. Then he went, and the beautiful music and accompanying angels also went. I had been a spectator in a very moving scene.

I wrote to the elderly lady when she left for the

hospice, and I believe my letter was a comfort to her husband when she died.

It was some time before I could tell the other patient what I had seen Jesus do for her and her family. I invited her to Women Aglow at Christmas 1995, and shared the special blessing I felt she had received. She said 'So long as none of my children was left out.' And, of course, no one is excluded by Jesus. Now she is a member of our church and of my home group, and going from strength to strength.

God is good!

This story is particularly interesting, featuring both the presence of the spiritual opposition, and a choir of angels. The testimony of my correspondent obviously brought spiritual blessing to the dying old lady, and appears to have helped the hospital sister become a Christian.

The old lady

My next story features a strange encounter which helped restore the faith and commitment of a young person. My correspondent is now at university:

When I was fourteen (exactly five years ago), I was going through a troubled time involving rebellion from my family, school and everything. I ceased to love God wholeheartedly and I lived a very dangerous, selfish and sinful life. My best friend at that time (whom I still speak to probably because we shared this experience) was an ardent atheist, perhaps because her father died when she was nine and because she is a sceptical person. For years I had tried to encourage her in her faith but failed. I don't think either of us would be here now if it weren't for God's mercy in sending us a sign of hope.

It happened that we were shopping in my hometown and decided to sit down on a bench to rest, there was an ugly old woman sitting there and we somehow began to talk with her. There was nothing peculiar about her except that she was very old looking, her face was unusually creased and she was plain, not a person one would normally take notice of. I will tell you now that the whole time we spent in her presence we were unaware of what was happening, we did not realise anything until after it was too late, hence we were unable to ask her the things we would have wanted to had we known what she was. We don't know how long we spent with her, time seemed to vanish – it was immaterial. I will also note here that my friend has never been able to talk about what happened with people since it upsets her, but I do not have this problem.

The first thing to note is that the old woman was a prophet. She knew things about us, for example she knew my friend had eating problems, which I myself had no notion of and it was in no way obvious from looking at her. She knew our names (we realised afterwards how strange this was since we referred to each other with pet names), she advised me about a boy I liked that he was very bad for me and would cause me pain – he nearly ruined my life! She also talked a great deal about God and about faith; how it is a gift, the greatest gift a person can have and that if you find it, to hold onto it and allow it to flourish and grow. She talked of heaven and God's love for humankind.

My memory does not recall all that she said but a few

things distinctly stand out. When we asked her what her career had been (forgetting that women in the twenties were usually housewives) she replied, 'I am a messenger from God'. At the time we assumed she meant a religious person who preaches his word, but reflecting on it afterwards we realised that the word *'messenger'* means *'angel'*. She also said, 'I may not be beautiful to look at but I am wise.' She was joyous that we had seen her, which I did think odd at the time, she said, 'I'm so glad that we have met today, I hope one day in your busy lives you will look back and remember me, it would be so nice.' I remember thinking that I am so cool and young that I doubt whether I really will ever remember her but I can honestly tell you now that rarely does a day pass that I don't think of her. She blessed us and prayed to the sky, 'praise you Lord, for I have brought two more of your lost flock to your kingdom' but we did not understand what she meant.

When we finally came to leave the bench she kissed us goodbye and told us that she loved us and that we were God's children, as we turned our back and took a few steps forward I looked at my friend and was startled. She was ghostly white and I said to her, 'are you all right, you look awful?' My friend stopped and stood still and said, 'I believe in God.' 'How can you' I asked. 'I'm so glad, why suddenly do you have faith?' She answered, 'Because you are my angel'. At that moment we both turned and looked at the bench. The old lady had vanished. We looked all around and said at the same time 'But little old ladies can't walk that fast' and we began to panic and weep.

There was a woman who had been standing near the bench watching us (I think she was waiting for us to leave the bench so that she could take our seats) and I approached her and asked, 'the old lady I was talking with just now, where did she go? Did you see her walk off?' And the woman looked at me and said, 'What old lady? I didn't see anyone.' We realised that no one had seen her except us, and she was as real to us as we are to each other.

Following this encounter, I went to boarding school and about six months to a year later I was touched by the Holy Spirit whilst in prayer and my faith has grown and is growing every day. I have achieved many prizes and awards and I do not think my life could be more rich and full than it is. I'm so lucky to have been set back on the right path since I am convinced that I would not be here to tell you this story now if it weren't for what happened that afternoon.

As well as at individual conversions, visions of angels and supernatural light have sometimes been seen just before times of great spiritual blessing.

Celestial light in Scotland

The revival in the Outer Hebrides began in 1949, as the Holy Spirit stirred up a few people to new heights of prayer. Two old sisters, Peggy and Christine Smith, had a particular burden for their island. They believed the promise written in Isaiah 44:3: 'For I will pour water on the thirsty land, and streams on the dry ground; I will pour out my Spirit on your offspring, and my blessing on your descendants.'

They often prayed far into the night, while seven church leaders in the parish of Barabhas met in a barn, and for many months prayed long and hard. Then it became obvious that all around people were praying. Lights could be seen in many buildings, far into the night. People started to sense God's power, there was a mighty wind, a sense of God's glory, and a supernatural light above many of the houses. The only proper response seemed to be that of the psalmist, 'Be still, and know that I am God' (Psalm 46:10).

One early morning, several hundred people, from a small and scattered community, were drawn to meet for prayer outside the community police station at 4 a.m! People were lying on the main road, crying out to God. It was as if the community was only concerned with the things of eternity. Many people were converted, and all who were involved had their faith, and expectation, deepened.

An angelic vision before a renewal

My friend Roger Simpson, now vicar of St Michael-le-Belfry in York, sent me this story concerning an earlier part of his ministry:

> I went to St Paul's and St George's in 1989. It was a large Episcopal church at the far end of Queen Street, right in the centre of Edinburgh. The church had fallen on hard times and had a congregation of between twenty and thirty. Another church called St Thomas' had invited me to plant a church into the city centre and they gave us fifty to sixty of their people. After we had been there about a month or two, and the congregation had already begun to grow rapidly, I had one of those encounters that you never forget.
>
> I had just baptized Duncan Campbell's[6] great-grandson at one of the morning services, and as I was standing on the door, an elderly lady said to me, 'I need to speak to

you.' I went to visit her the next day. She lived in a very posh flat in Herriot Row, and she told me the most amazing story. She had come back from India with her husband after the war, and they had gone to live in the family home on the Isle of Skye. While there, her husband had died, and the Episcopal priest who visited them on the island was from St Paul's and St George's. As a result, she moved to Edinburgh, joined the church, and over the next fifteen years she saw the congregation get smaller and smaller.

The priest was very discouraged, and during one Evensong (she told me that there were about nine people in the congregation), in the middle of the prayers, she looked up in this huge church, and she saw many, many angels hovering over the church. There was tremendous brightness and glory, and then 'in the Spirit', she saw hundreds of people crowding to get into the church. Then the vision passed. She stayed in that church for another ten years, and eventually the congregation had to move into the little chapel underneath the nave. She thought she was going mad, but she carried on praying. After the vicar left, she then went away to the Isle of Skye. She came back a year and a half later, and stood on the pavement, with all the students who were queuing to get into the church! She wept and wept. Her vision was fulfilled, and the church grew over the next seven years to 800 people.

That remarkable vision inspired one faithful elderly woman to pray. Many other churches have become alive partly through the faithful prayers of elderly members. Roger Simpson's ministry has been greatly blessed. His experience in Edinburgh was very important both to him and to his congregation. Here, as so often occurs, there is a beautiful mingling of God's sovereign purpose, which was revealed in the angelic vision, faithful prayer and evangelistic preaching.

The miracle of conversion

Every conversion, each rebirth of a dead church, each revival, whether or not it is accompanied by supernatural signs, is a miracle. Jesus made that clear when at the end of his perplexing conversation with Nicodemus, he said: 'The wind blows wherever it pleases. You hear its sound, but you cannot tell where it comes from or where it is going. So it is with everyone born of the Spirit' (John 3:8).

The apostles understood this when they prayed for boldness, signs and wonders. Their prayers were answered by a supernatural shaking of the building (see Acts 4:23–31).

Recently I listened to Michael Cassidy preaching in Bath. After all the miracles in South Africa surrounding the dismantling of apartheid[7] he was somewhat pessimistic of the current state of affairs. Miracles, visions and signs have to be sustained by hard work, and a continued openness to God's more normal means of grace. He did however strike an optimistic note, with an account of a visit to a predominately Muslim country, where the Christians were engaging in fervent prayer. There had been some remarkable conversions – mainly of Muslims who had dreams and visions of the risen Christ.

Soon after writing these words, a missionary visiting our church told me this story:

A devoted Indonesian Muslim on his third pilgrimage to Mecca was travelling with a party of others in a coach.

As they drove along from Mecca to Medina he started talking to the coach driver. When the driver discovered that the Indonesian was on his third pilgrimage, he remarked that this must have cost him a great deal of money. On being assured that it was indeed very expensive to come on the pilgrimage, the driver went on to ask why the Indonesian didn't give his money to the poor instead, as the Christians do!

The Indonesian was so surprised that he didn't know what to say. Later that day he told others about this strange conversation. When they heard it, they became very angry because they were sure that the driver must have been a Christian, and a Christian was not allowed to be among them, for otherwise their pilgrimage could lose its value! However, when the driver was called to reassure them that he was a Muslim, the Indonesian was even more confused, as the coach driver – whom all the other passengers recognized – was not the man he had been talking to that day in the coach.

The Indonesian returned home still in a state of confusion over the incident. Some time later, he was visiting the home of a Christian friend and saw a picture on the wall, which he recognized as that of the 'coach driver'. When he asked who this man was, he was told that the picture was of Jesus. As a result of this experience, the man, and about fifty of his relatives and friends, came to faith in Christ.

For obvious reasons, I have given no identification of the source or the people involved. Christians are facing terrible persecution in parts of Indonesia. There is a great spiritual battle taking place there. Intense prayer is being accompanied by remarkable signs, and persecutions. Our visitor told us of young Christians refusing to deny Jesus and dying for their faith, of churches being destroyed, and yet of much growth in holiness and evangelism. In another part of world, an even more powerful spiritual encounter was taking place.

The voice of God and the Muslim leader

Conversion to Christianity is very costly for people of other faiths – especially Muslims. But sometimes God speaks so clearly – even more clearly than by the sending of an angel – that there seems to be no choice. This testimony was written for me by a prominent Anglican, who is involved in the work of mission and renewal, and who has heard 'A' speak and had met him. For obvious reasons, we have omitted personal and geographical details. 'A' gave this testimony:

I was trained at the Egyptian Islamic University in Sharia law. Then I returned to my home country to study international law at the leading university. Because I was a radical Muslim, I was being groomed as a future leader and was working amongst international Muslim students. I had the title of Imam in the university mosque. I became a Christian on Friday 2nd September 2001. I had been leading a Muslim prayer meeting. My heart was strong for Islam. We followed the teachings of the Qu'ran and gave converts money; there was also a deliberate process of impregnating Christian girls – who then produced children who would grow up as Muslims. I was very tired – I had coursework to write up on my legal studies. I hid away in a quiet room, recited the Qu'ran and fell asleep while reading my law books. I was woken up by a great wind which was followed with echoes. I heard a voice calling my name three times. The voice said 'I am the Lord – I want you to get saved.' This agreed with what I had heard when having conversations with Christians in Egypt and other places.

I went out to the mosque. I was very angry and I went to take my ritual ablutions. I came back to pray. I emphasized that I was a radical Muslim. As I was still praying, the voice called me again. The walls shook. Glass broke in the windows, and many people ran out of the mosque. Others stayed with me. The voice continued 'I am the Lord – Christ Jesus – I want you to get saved.' My heart was very certain that it was God speaking to me because part of my prayer had been that he would make it clear to me what he was saying. I had prayed to Allah and this seemed to be the answer. I could not become a Christian. I would be killed, I would be unable to finish my legal studies and it would betray all my family. They were all staunch Muslims. Shame would fall on my people. I tried to bargain with God. I asked him to give me a year to finish my degree. As I did so, a light came accompanied by great heat. I saw a scroll pictured on the wall. As it unrolled, I read Psalm 56. I rushed out of the mosque. I ran into a Christian church. I found a number of Christians and asked how I could be saved. There were a large group of men and women praying. Men and women together – that was impossible for a Muslim. Worse still, they were wearing shoes. I had no idea where to sit. The whole church stopped praying when they discovered what was happening. They broke out in spontaneous praise to God. They cried out 'the great Sheik has become a Christian!' I gave my testimony. They said 'God has called you!' I confessed Jesus Christ as my saviour. I added 'Christ has brought me to lose everything. I have gone from being a Muslim leader to just being a brother.'

I have lost a lot – that is why I am so serious about it. Soon afterwards I told my girlfriend that I had become a Christian. She told my family, who were astounded. The next day, I was asked to go to the mosque. My family put great pressure on me. I went through the ritual ablutions, but prayed that I would not have to go to the mosque, because I was frightened about returning there. I had a great sense of power and heat. It felt as though I had a fever, people were concerned for my health and I didn't have to go to the mosque. The next day, I told them in the mosque and in my home that I had become a Christian.

My father slapped me and told me to leave home immediately. He said he ought to kill me but that he loved me too much to do that. A Roman Catholic student friend took me into his room because I was now homeless. Later at an international event, journalists wanted to interview me. A little while later, some Muslims shot and killed a friend of mine – mistaking him for me. I am covered with both Christ's and my friend's blood. The murderers were caught and imprisoned; but I have become a foreigner in my own country. Christian brothers and sisters have given me money and lodgings. Others tried to assassinate me. Some came from Libya and Egypt. Twice I was shot, in my stomach and in my leg. But despite being in a coma for two weeks, I have survived. I am now studying at a Bible college in England – financed by a Christian missionary organization.

All true conversions are miracles of grace. God challenges people in a variety of ways. More normal encounters occur through prayer, worship, reading the Bible, the testimony of friends, preaching, acts of kindness... In this chapter, we have been hearing the stories of people who have encountered God through the appearance of angels, or in dreams, visions and by hearing celestial voices. Such encounters are *highly unusual*. Within the sovereign will of God, these encounters have taken place. Doubtless such unusual means of conversion will continue to happen until the end of time.

Notes

1. *Augustine Confessions Book Ten*, chapter XLII. For his conversion see *Book Eight*. Augustine on miracles, see *City of God, Books 8–10*. Translated by H. Bettenson, London: Penguin, 1984 and Bede, *A History of the English Church and People*, translated by Leo Sherley-Price, London: Penguin, 1955, pp.120ff. Also John Woolmer, *Angels*, Oxford: Monarch, 2003, pp. 120–23.
2. See any standard life of Sundar Singh. I am grateful for the summary of his life in David Shrisunder's *Encounters with Angels* 1995, obtainable from the author by e-mail at Shrisunder@abbeypress.net.
3. Transformations Videos are produced by the Sentinel Group, and distributed by Gateway Christian Media Ltd., PO 11905, London NW10 4ZQ. Both the revival amongst the Eskimos and the revival in the Hebrides appear in great detail.
4. See Fred Smith, *God's Gift of Healing*, New Wine Press, 1986.
5. Fred Lemon, *Breakout*, Lakeland, 1977.
6. Duncan Campbell was the evangelist who, humanly, was used as the evangelist in 1949 in the Outer Hebrides. For other stories about revival, prayer and visions, see Dr Mark Stibbe, *Thinking Clearly about Revival*, Oxford: Monarch, 1998.
7. See, amongst others of his writings: Michael Cassidy, *A Witness For Ever*, London: Hodder & Stoughton, 1995.

CHAPTER 6

Angels in Conflict

T HE CLAIM THAT God sometimes intervenes, through his angels, in human conflicts seems, to many, more appropriate to the myths of ancient Greece and Rome, than to the history of the Christian era.

However, the evidence of Scripture, ancient and modern history, is sufficiently powerful to make a strong case. The Old Testament is unequivocal; the New Testament (especially the book of Revelation) sees a continuous battle mainly in the heavenly realms; early Christian history tells of the surprising conversion of Constantine – widely attributed to a sign that he saw in the sky before a crucial battle; modern history produces persistent stories of angelic encounters attributed to a wide range of people – George Washington in the midst of the American War of Independence, British soldiers in the First World War, widely attested stories from recent war zones and potential war zones in Rhodesia, Vietnam and South Africa. In Chapter 2, we included recent testimony from Bougainville, a troubled island off Papua New Guinea.

We look at some of these, starting with recent history, then touching on some of the many stories relating to the events in the First World War and moving back to events vividly recorded in the Old Testament. Recent world history has been shaped by the destruction of the Twin Towers in New York on 11 September 2001. As well as the dramatic political fall-out, there have been some interesting spiritual consequences.

An angel in Pakistan?

One of the many results of the attack on 11 September, coupled with the American-led military response in Afghanistan
and Iraq, has been an enormous increase in tension between
Christians and Muslims. In England, many Muslims have
felt unwelcome and some have suffered physical attack; in
Pakistan there have been several examples of murderous
attacks on Christian churches and schools. In July 2002, the
Christian school at Murree[1], which mainly teaches the children of missionaries, was attacked by terrorists. The attack
was carefully premeditated and ingenious. The fastest way
to remove missionaries from the country would have been to
kill their children. The attack went wrong. Despite the tragic
death of six Pakistanis (some Christian, some Muslim) there
seems to have been a remarkable amount of protection. If
the terrorists had come ten minutes earlier, they would have
found the whole school out playing during their break. As it
was, they were back in their classes. Though the attackers
had grenades, they did not use them. When they tried to
enter the classrooms, they failed (for no adequate reason –
one door was locked and they failed to open it, but didn't
notice a nearby door that was open). When they had shot
the guards and run through the property, and had everything at their mercy, they inexplicably ran away. One parent
was shot in the hand, but was then directed to safety by two
large men in an unknown uniform who seem to have been
angels – no soldiers of that description have been traced,
and the uniform that the parent described is unknown in
Pakistan. Apparently, the terrorists were trapped crossing a
river. Pursued by local soldiers, and opposed by villagers on
the opposite bank, they apparently blew themselves up.

This incident raises, even more sharply, a familiar question. If God intervened directly to protect the children, why were six people, all doing their duty, killed? Why is angelic intervention sometimes partial? This type of question is unanswerable. We have a choice – we can reject any idea of God intervening (as many theologians and others did after the terrible Tsunami on 26 December 2004) or we can admit that the evidence for God's involvement is very strong and accept that our understanding is partial. Paul, with his customary wisdom, wrote: 'now we see through a glass, darkly' (1 Corinthians 13:12, AV).

11 September 2001

The destruction of the World Trade Center in New York by suicide bombers gave the American people, and their friends in the Western world, their biggest shock for many years. The events unleashed a whole series of responses, the outcome of which is completely unpredictable. People could ask: where were the guardian angels?

We know that many people were killed (though many fewer than through the eruption of the volcano near Goma in Congo a few months later). We know that many professing Christians were among the victims. We know that a number of Christians had warnings that something was about to happen. One relief worker had dreams of a huge disaster, and a sense that he would be called to work in Afghanistan, something that seemed highly unlikely before 11 September. When I was in Nairobi in December 2001, I was told that a Kenyan had telephoned his mother on 10 September to say that he was now willing to go anywhere that the Lord called him – the next day he was among the victims. That last phone call gave great comfort to his family.

On 11 September, Sujo John reached work at 7.30 a.m. His new place of work was in an office on the eighty-first floor of the World Trade Center's north tower. At 8.04, he sent a friend an e-mail saying, 'I have a call of God on my life', adding that he needed to do more than merely attend church each Sunday.

At 8.45 a.m. one of the hijacked planes hit the north tower; one wing sliced through his floor killing several of his colleagues. He joined the flight down the stairs, passing the brave firemen running up. On the fifty-third floor, he tried, unsuccessfully, to telephone his wife. She was pregnant with their first child, and was coming into work at the south tower. At 9.03 the second plane hit the south tower, almost exactly where she worked. Sujo reached the base of the tower, and was just about to exit through a revolving door, when the whole building collapsed.

He was trapped with about fifteen other terrified people. As the building collapsed, he shouted to them, inspired by his deepened commitment to Christ, 'We're going to die. Do you know the Lord? Call upon the Lord and you will be saved!' People started crying out, 'Jesus, Jesus'. He was trapped for about twenty minutes; he expected to be killed at any moment. The others didn't survive, but Sujo said, 'I felt the peace of God as never before, because I knew they were in a better place.' He was trapped under about three feet of dust and debris, and could hardly breathe, but amidst the dense smoke and fumes, he spotted the torch-light of a man in a FBI jacket who was prone, but still alive. They both thought they were going to die.

Together, they started to pray, and as they did so, they

spotted through the gloom the flashing red light of an ambulance. When, somehow, they reached the ambulance, they found that half of it had been crushed. Sujo believed that God had placed that flashing light to show them a way out. He left the disaster without a scratch, convinced that his wife and unborn child would have been killed in the other half of the disaster.

In fact, his wife had arrived for work just after the second tower was hit, and found her way to work barred. If she had arrived a few minutes earlier, she would almost certainly have been killed.[2]

Sujo has learnt from his experience, and is now preaching to thousands, helping a grieving nation turn back to their God for salvation, comfort and guidance. As I write this, my mind goes back to the King's Cross tube disaster nearly twenty-five years earlier. A young man called Lionel, a Christian in a very strongly Christian family, was killed there. I used to know him well; he was a member of a youth group that I had run in a previous church. There will always be these paradoxes.

More angels in recent history

In the period after World War Two, there have been many bloody conflicts. Events in Vietnam, the Congo and Zimbabwe have been amongst the most violent. My friend John Knight[3] tells of two similar incidents which occurred in the late 1970s when he was working as a priest in Zimbabwe (Rhodesia, as it was then).

Military intelligence had learnt that the largest ever guerilla force to enter Zimbabwe was about to cross into the country in our area – a densely forested and mountainous area. Many small 'details' or 'sticks' of men were out searching for signs of this group. A young Christian we knew, and his friend, formed a two-man stick, with radio, and were searching through their allotted section. They came over a hill and were well down the slope before realising that the thick undergrowth of the valley floor was 'crawling' with men. They had unexpectedly walked into the hide-out of nearly a thousand guerillas who had with them a small mountain of war material.

At the same moment, they too were spotted, and a battle royal ensued. Our two young friends could only do one thing – dive into a small contour on the hillside, and start returning the fire. They started praying. Their radio was not picking up any friends. In moments, the three or four magazines they each had for their weapons were expended.

They knew that only God could help them now. All of a sudden, they realised that all the shooting had stopped. Looking carefully out of their meagre hiding place, they were scarcely able to believe what met their eyes. The large group was moving swiftly back towards the border, leaving much of the heaviest material behind. In subsequent follow-up operations, one man was caught and interrogated. Amongst other things, they asked why the group had run off down the valley. The guerilla explained that when they saw the whole hillside 'alive' with soldiers in white uniforms, they knew that they were heavily outnumbered, and so made a run for it!

On another occasion when these 'soldiers in white'

appeared, they brought protection to an elderly couple living in a lonely homestead. Feeling a little more nervous this particular evening, the couple knelt down to pray as usual before going to bed, and asked that God's angels would protect them from danger. In the early hours of the following morning a guerrilla band attacked a neighbouring homestead a couple of miles away, and met with more than they bargained for. It was occupied by security force personnel!

In the battle that followed, the security forces took, as a prisoner, one of the men they wounded. In the interrogation that followed, the guerrilla explained that they had decided to attack the neighbouring farmstead, but when they got there, they found it surrounded and heavily guarded by soldiers in white, so they abandoned their first plan and moved against the homestead that – unbeknown to them – was actually guarded by the security forces!

Gill Farrow, who worked as a nurse for twenty-five years in Rhodesia/Zimbabwe told me of a number of incidents – some of protection, some of tragedy. Here is some of her testimony:

In the Vumba, in the mountainous area of the Eastern Highlands, thick mists can come down very suddenly, reducing visibility to almost nil. Three young white Rhodesian soldiers, on active service, were caught in such a mist. They were crouching in the shelter of some rocks waiting for the mist to clear. Suddenly, there was a gap in the mist; they were able to see young black guerrilla soldiers also caught in the mist. They were about to open fire when they saw that the black soldiers were reading a Bible. Instead of firing, they broke cover and approached the black soldiers, saying that they, too, were Christians. The black and white soldiers prayed together. They went their separate ways. Were guardian angels involved? – I think so!

In the war years, I was often alone with my children. As things got more dangerous, the last thing that I did at night was to take out a gun, load it and put it on the bedside table. One night as I did this, I told God that I really trusted him to look after us! God must have a sense of humour. With total clarity, I 'heard' in my mind the words 'Then put the gun back in the drawer'. I never took it out again when my husband was away – and I felt much safer!

Years later, I was feeling very unsafe walking in Harare. I was the only white person in a sea of black Zimbabweans. I was near the army barracks, a place that I felt very uncomfortable about and it was very hot, about 40 degrees centigrade. A man was walking towards me. He had a coat over his arm which was concealing a gun. As we drew level, I heard the click of the safety catch being released. Suddenly, I found myself looking down the barrel of a gun. It all happened very quickly, and I felt that I was moved sideways. The man looked at me and said 'Sorry'. What did he see? Why did he walk away? I associate this incident, and other incidents of protection, with the obedience that I had offered God when I put my loaded gun away in the bedroom and trusted him for protection.

During the war years, a woman was in the kitchen on a farm outside Bulawayo. She, a Christian, was suddenly overwhelmed with fear. She knelt down on the kitchen floor to pray. As long as she knelt, the fear lifted, but if she tried to get up, the fear flooded back. A security patrol came by. They found an armed guerrilla sitting up in a tree overlooking the farm. They asked him why he hadn't shot the woman which had been his obvious intention. He said that he had been unable to do so because there was a huge soldier, dressed in white, guarding her.

We, as a family, were living in a Christian farm community, deep in the bush in a dangerous place outside Bulawayo. In post-independence Zimbabwe, many Matabele people felt they had missed out under Mugabe's Mashona-led government. As a result, many former freedom fighters had gone back into the bush to fight as dissidents. Mugabe had sent his much feared Fifth Brigade, who had been trained by North Koreans, to hunt them down. There was much cruelty and civilians were frequently caught in the midst of it all. An estimated 30,000 were killed in this part of the unfolding tragedy in Zimbabwe.

One of the children on the farm had a dream about one of us being ambushed. In her dream, she saw two huge angels one on each side of the car deflecting bullets. Marian, her mother, told her not to talk about it as it could make people afraid. Two weeks after Deborah's dream, I was ambushed in the exact place which she had seen in her dream. Four dissidents were firings AKs. The car was hit seventeen times (my son counted the holes). I was not hit. During the hail of bullets, the phrase 'but it will not come near you' (Psalm 91:7b) came into my mind. I was able to call out one word – Jesus. The car lost speed and I thought that the engine had been damaged. I was trying to escape and drive round a bend. The quiet instruction 'change gear' came into my mind. As I did so, the car picked up speed. One tyre had been shot away, and I drove some 18 kilometres on a stony bush track, until I reached the relative safety of the tarmac road leading to Bulawayo.

After this happened, Deborah told me about her dream. She mentioned how in the dream the high (her word) angels were deflecting the bullets. Of course, I asked the unanswerable question – why when others were being killed was I saved?

Debora was massacred some time later with the rest of the community. I heard how close they had all become to the Lord and to each other before it happened. The white members of the farm community, sixteen of them including a six-week-old baby and Deborah, who was now aged sixteen, were massacred while the black members of the community were made to watch. The dissidents, high on drink and drugs, came one night.

At the time, I was back in England working at the Burrswood Christian Healing Centre and was in Eastbourne on the day that it happened. When I returned, David Flagg the senior chaplain contacted me. He took me to his home, and he and his wife prayed for me. I was immediately aware that I was surrounded by shafts of light. I knew it was to do with the community in Zimbabwe, but was puzzled by the shafts of light.

Sometime later, I returned to Zimbabwe and went to the farm where I spent time with Thembe, one of the black community members. He had witnessed everything that happened. There were two farms then, and the dissidents gathered the white people from each farm. They made them sit in a circle with their hands tied behind their backs with barbed wire. Deborah, who had the dream about my protection, asked her father how she should pray. Gerry, her father, said 'Pray that they (the killers) should know Jesus.'

They were called out, one by one starting with a fourteen-year-old girl, called Glynis[4], to be killed with an axe. Deborah was one of those killed. Thembe told me that no one was afraid, not even the children. It was as though they were already with the Lord before they were killed. He said that as each one died, a shaft of light came down on the victim and then lifted. The killers saw this. They were disturbed but went on with the massacre. They taunted some of the adults before killing them. They said to Deborah's father 'We are your Jesus now!' He replied that he was going to be with Jesus.

Thembe told me that shafts of light were seen descending and ascending as each one died. He also said that villages sixty miles away had seen light over the whole area where the farms were.

What was happening? I am sure that the shafts of light, which I also sensed when I heard the news in England, indicated the presence of angels. The martyrdom of Stephen recorded in Acts 6 and 7 has parallels. Luke, the author of Acts, writes that 'his face was like the face of an angel' (Acts 6:15). We also know that Saul of Tarsus, later to become Paul the great missionary, was present 'giving approval to his death'. Was there a future Christian missionary amongst the Zimbabwean murderers? It wouldn't be unusual[5].

Moving further back in history, the First World War produced many accounts of angelic intervention. Some of these are remarkably well documented.

Angels in the First World War

The First World War was perhaps the most bloodthirsty, and unnecessary, event in the history of the human race. The terrible experiences in the trenches, and the ultimate humiliation of Germany in the Treaty of Versailles, had other devastating consequences.

Theologians, and ordinary people, lost faith in the God revealed in Scripture. This precipitated a decline in Western Christendom, which continues unabated even today. The people of Germany welcomed Adolf Hitler to restore their fortunes. But amidst the carnage of the war, there were many stories of angels.

From the British side, there are an incredible number of accounts of angels being seen amidst the horrors of the First World War. Of course, any such accounts raise huge questions. But the evidence is well documented. One of the most striking, and least well known, occurred very near the end of the war. In the spring of 1918, the Germans tried to end the war with a massive assault. They broke through, and the Allied troops were retreating in disarray. *The Household Brigade Magazine* describes what happened as follows[6]:

A senior German officer gave the following extraordinary account of the events: The order had been given to advance in mass formation, and our troops were marching behind us singing their way to victory, when Fritz, my lieutenant here, said, 'Herr Kapitan, just look at that open ground behind Bethune. There is a brigade of cavalry coming up through the smoke drifting across it! They must be mad, these Englishmen, to advance against such a force as ours in the open! I suppose they must be cavalry of one of their Colonial Forces, for look! They're all in white uniforms and are mounted on white horses!'

'Strange,' I said, 'I've never heard of English having any white cavalry whether Colonial or not. Anyway, they've all been fighting on foot for several years past, and in khaki, not white.' 'Well, they're plain enough,' he replied. 'But look! Our guns have got them in their range now, they'll be blown to pieces in no time.'

We actually saw the shells bursting among the horses and their riders which still came forward at a quiet walk, in parade-ground formation, each man and horse in his exact place. Shortly afterwards our machine guns opened a heavy fire, raking the advancing cavalry with a hail of lead; but they still came, and not a single man or horse fell. Steadily they advanced, clear in the shining sunlight, and a few paces in front of them rode their leader, a fine figure of a man, whose hair, like spun gold, shone in an aura around his head. By his side was a great sword, but his hands lay quietly holding the reins, as his huge white charger bore him proudly forward. In spite of heavy shelling and concentrated machine-gun fire, the white cavalry advanced remorselessly as fate, like the incoming tide on a sandy beach. Then a great fear fell over me. I turned to flee; yes, I, an officer of the Prussian Guard, fled panic stricken, and around me were hundreds of terrified men, whimpering like children, throwing away their weapons and accoutrements in order not to have their movements impeded... all running. Their one desire was to get away from that advancing white cavalry, but above all from their awe-inspiring leader whose hair shone like a golden aureole... we are beaten by the white cavalry... I cannot understand... I cannot understand.

During the days that followed, many German prisoners were examined and their account tallied in substance with the one given here. From the British side, the whole event seemed inexplicable. They didn't see any white cavalry, with or without riders. But they did see, and hear, the Germans start firing at a completely empty area of open ground, then a sudden panic amidst the well-drilled, disciplined Germans, followed by the complete cessation of a shattering bombardment.

Elisha's servant (see 2 Kings 6:8 and the end of the chapter) could have enlightened both sides!

The Second World War

There are a number of other stories of small nations being protected by angels at times of great difficulty. Certainly in Finland, in 1939, against all the odds, the Finnish army repulsed the might of the invading Soviet Union. There are a number of persistent stories about angels assisting in the battle. Dr Moolenburgh[7] also tells a story of a German invasion into neutral Switzerland being stopped supernaturally in May 1940.

While there are many fewer documented stories from the Second World War, there is also a deep sense that Britain's survival in 1940 was due to prevailing prayer, and some unusual events.

The shattering defeat of the British Expeditionary Force ought to have been followed by its capture and annihilation on the beaches of Dunkirk. For some reason, Hitler failed to give the order to attack, and an extraordinary combination of calm weather and cool heads enabled thousands of small boats to rescue the stranded army. Your writer's father was amongst those rescued.

The Battle of Britain, fought in the air in August and September in 1940, was similarly a victory against all the odds. Strange stories were told of supernatural intervention. According to Billy Graham, Air Chief Marshall Lord Dowding, who was in charge of the operation, believed the victory was miraculous, and that angels had sometimes been directly involved. Without that victory, England would certainly have been invaded, and in all probability would have had to negotiate a humiliating peace.

Going much further back in history there is a fascinating account of an angelic visitation to George Washington. This occurred at a critical time when the war of independence, fought against Britain the then colonial power, was going badly.

An angel in America

In the winter of 1777, after a series of military defeats, George Washington, the American leader in the War of Independence fought against England, was in despair. This account of what happened is abridged from an account given by one of his staff officers, Anthony Sherman. Sherman, a youth of eighteen at the time, told the story many years later at an Independence Day parade in 1858. He was then ninety-nine years old[8]!

One day – I remember it well – when the bitterly cold wind was whistling through the leafless trees, and the sun shone brightly in a cloudless sky, he stayed in his room on his own all afternoon. When he came outside I noticed that his face was paler than usual, his soul seemed to be full of something of extraordinary importance. Dusk was falling when he sent a servant to the rooms of the officer of the guard with a request to come to him. When he arrived we talked for about half an hour and then Washington said to us: 'I do not know whether it is because of my anxiety, or something else, but this afternoon, as I was sitting at my table writing an urgent report there was something in the room that disturbed me. I looked up and saw an extremely beautiful woman standing opposite me. Because I had given strict orders that I was not to be disturbed I was so surprised that it was a while before I could utter a word to ask her why she was there. I repeated my question a second, third and even fourth time, but my mysterious guest gave no answer, except to slightly raise her eyes. At the same time a strange feeling made it impossible for me to do anything. Once again I tried to speak to her but I had lost my tongue, even my mind was paralyzed. A new influence mysterious, powerful, irresistible, took possession of me. The only thing I could do was to stare at my unknown visitor steadily, without moving.

'I did not think, I was only conscious of staring fixedly and mindlessly at my guest. Then I heard a voice say: "Son of the Republic, look and learn!"'

There followed three detailed visions, each of which was proceeded by the solemn words, 'Son of the Republic, look and learn!' The first concerned the War of Independence. The second, clearly, concerns the Civil War (1861–65). Sherman's account of it given just before the Civil War started was as follows:

I turned my gaze to America and saw villages and towns and cities appearing one by one until they were scattered over the entire country from the Atlantic Ocean to the Pacific Ocean. Then the dark, shadowy angel turned his face to the south and I saw an ominous ghost approaching our country from Africa. He glided slowly and heavily over every town and city and then the inhabitants prepared for battle against each other. As I looked I saw a shining angel bearing a crown of light with the word 'Union'. He carried the American flag which he placed between the people of the divided nation and said: 'Remember that you are brothers.' Immediately the inhabitants threw down their arms and made friends, united under the national banner.

The third vision consisted of a colossal, and unexpected, attack on the land of America. Eventually, it concluded with the words:

The dark cloud rolled back together with the armies which it had brought with it, leaving the inhabitants of the land victorious. Again I saw how villages, towns and cities arose where they had formerly been, while the shining angel planted the banner he had brought with him among them and called out in a loud voice: 'As long as the stars continue to exist and the dew falls on earth from heaven, the Republic will go on.' He took the crown from his head with the word 'Union' flashing on it and placed it on the banner, while the people knelt down and said, 'Amen.'

Straight away the scene started to blur and dissolve and finally I saw only the swirling mist rising up as I had seen in the beginning. When this also disappeared I once again gazed upon the mysterious visitor who said in the same voice I had heard at first: 'Son of the Republic, what you have seen is explained as follows: The Republic will suffer three great disasters. The most terrible is the second of these and when it is past the whole of the world together will not be able to triumph over it. Let every child of the Republic learn to live for his God, his country and the Union.' With these words he vanished and I stood up from my chair and felt that I had seen a vision which showed me the birth, the progress and the destiny of the United States.

The first part of the vision encouraged George Washington, a deeply prayerful man, at the darkest time in the great struggle against England; the second was about the ghastly Civil War, which was mainly fought over the question of the abolition of slavery. The ghost from Africa presumably refers to the slave trade, which caused so much suffering, and so tarnished the Christian cause in America. The third is hard to interpret. America is so strong, that an invasion seems all but impossible – unless of course the vision pre-saged the events on and beyond 11 September 2001. There are, not surprisingly, an extraordinary number of stories surrounding that tragic day (see above).

There are also stories from more ancient times, notably recorded by Bede[9], but we conclude this chapter with an archetypal account from the Old Testament recorded in 2 Kings 6:8ff. The king of Aram, infuriated by the prophet Elisha's supernatural knowledge of his plans, sent an army to capture him. Early one morning, Elisha's servant discovered that the city where they were living was now surrounded by a large army. In a panic, he alerted his master. The prophet had a simple reply: 'Don't be afraid... Those who are with us are more than those who are with them.' Elisha then prayed for his servant's eyes to be opened, and then the servant was able to see 'the hills full of horses and chariots of fire'. The end was unusually peaceful. The men of Aram were tem-porarily blinded, led into the city of Samaria, given food, and sent home with their vision restored. As we have seen there are a number of modern parallels to this story. We should also remember that the mysterious book of Revelation, the final book of the Bible, is full of angelic battles which will take place at the end of time as we understand it. Paul reminds us that much that goes on is unseen by most of us:

For our struggle is not against flesh and blood, but against the rulers, against the authorities, against the powers of this dark world and against the spiritual forces of evil in the heavenly realms. (Ephesians 6:12)

However, Paul, himself no stranger to visions (see 2 Corinthians 12:1–6, Acts 18:9 etc.), also writes this classic warning:

> Do not let anyone who delights in false humility and the worship of angels disqualify you for the prize. Such a person goes into great detail about what he has seen, and his unspiritual mind puffs him up with idle notions. (Colossians 2:18)

Jesus, strengthened by an angel in the Garden of Gethsemane (Luke 22:43) shortly afterwards declared to those who came to arrest him:

> Do you not think I cannot call on my Father, and he will put at my disposal more than twelve legions of angels? (Matthew 26:53)

Significantly, Jesus chose not to call on the angels. They were certainly available. Angels are all around us, but we like Elisha's servant need our eyes opening if we are to see or to sense them. The Bible, however, does not encourage us *to actively seek* these experiences.

Notes

1. I am indebted to Michael and Rosemary Green for this account. They visited Pakistan shortly after this incident to attend their son's ordination by the Bishop of Lahore. Their grandchildren were amongst those who escaped from the tragedy at the school.

   It is important to note that moderate followers of Islam helped to protect the children, and to corner the terrorists. In many parts of the world religious extremists, whether Hindu, Sikh, Muslim, Jewish or Christian, use the banner of their religion to promote evil acts.

Such conduct is always based on a narrow interpretation of their holy texts, and fuelled by perceived injustice to their fellow religionists. One of many obvious examples would be the sufferings of the Muslims, and the Christian minority, in the Palestinian refugee camps. Political and practical injustice in Palestine, coupled with a particular understanding of the Koran, is the seedbed for recruitment to the cause of the Islamic freedom fighters. Mix that with the dangerous teaching that death in a religious cause earns a place in Paradise, and a lethal spiritual cocktail has been concocted.

2. This account is based on Martin Fletcher's report in *The Times*, Saturday 24 November 2001.

3. John Knight, *Rain in a Dry Land*, London: Hodder & Stoughton, 1987, pp. 134ff.

4. Glynis was a close friend of my correspondent's daughter. They met in Bulawayo just three weeks before the massacre. Gill remembers her aged ten as someone with a remarkable awareness of God's presence and an extraordinary understanding of the Bible. It was as though God had put her on her an accelerated learning course knowing that her life would be short.

5. John Knight, *Ibid;* (John tells the story of another horrible massacre of Pentecostal missionaries where a number of the murderers were converted to Christianity – mainly due to their calm forgiving attitude. At least one became a missionary).

6. Dr Victor Pearce, *Miracles and Angels*, Surrey: Eagle, 1999, pp. 131ff. Based on an original document from *The Household Brigade Magazine*.

7. Dr H.C. Moolenburgh, *Meetings with Angels*, C.W. Daniel, 1992, pp. 147–8.

8. Dr H.C. Moolenburgh, *Ibid.* p. 138f. He makes the point that the American magazine *Destiny* regularly republishes this significant story. I have abridged his account.

9. See, for instance, Bede, *Ecclestiastical History of the English People* translated by Leo Sherley-Price, London: Penguin, 1955, pp. 27, 62, 144.

CHAPTER 7

Angels at the Gates of Eternity

IN THIS CHAPTER, we look at the testimonies of people, from the distant past and from recent times, who have had encounters with God at the point of apparent death, and the way that this has influenced the rest of their lives.

A friend who is member of a respected Anglican church shared this story with me. He was visiting a friend who was very ill. He read Psalm 91 at his bedside. He emphasizes verse 4: 'He will cover you with his feathers, and under his wings you find refuge; his faithfulness will be your shield and rampart' and verse 11 'For he will command his angels concerning you to guard you in all your ways'.

> When I read this, we both looked up. We both saw an angel in white with outstretched wings hovering briefly in the corner of the hospital bedroom. We were momentarily speechless. Then I completed the reading of the psalm and we prayed together.

He writes: 'I believe sometimes angels appear when God wants to emphasize a certain point in his word, for encouragement and comfort. I believe such was the case at that time. My friend died shortly afterwards.' I think this is fairly typical of such encounters; although some are rather more dramatic.

The Bible and the vision of Paradise

'The last enemy to be destroyed is death' (1 Corinthians 15:26). This confident statement comes in the middle of Paul's great chapter on the evidence for the resurrection of Jesus, with its profound implications for all his readers. But what happens beyond death? Over the centuries, people of different faiths have struggled with this question. Fascination with the afterlife has led many to seek solace in spiritualism; others have been comforted with beliefs in various forms of reincarnation; many have been driven to reject any belief in God (sometimes on the grounds that the afterlife sounds impossibly boring); a minority, recognizing the seriousness of God's call, have been inspired to evangelize the lost, sometimes in inhospitable distant quarters of the earth and sometimes in their own backyard.

The Bible contains many visions and deep spiritual experiences. Of these the ones that are most relevant to our subject are Paul's great vision of Paradise, and the book of Revelation. Paul describes his vision using the words 'whether it was in the body or out of the body I do not know – God knows', and gives us a glimpse of the wonder and beauty of Paradise. Paul didn't write much, saying that he 'heard inexpressible things, things that man is not permitted to tell' (see 2 Corinthians 12:1–10).

The book of Revelation is an extended vision given to the writer who 'on the Lord's Day was in the Spirit' (Revelation 1:10). Amongst many other things, this mysterious, and often misinterpreted, book gives us a wonderful picture of the worship of angels, and saints, in heaven (see chapters 4 and 5, especially), a description of the intense battle in the heavenly realms (chapter 12 and elsewhere) and a grim view of the second death and the lake of fire (chapter 20). It finishes with an electrifying vista of the radiance of the new Jerusalem, with the crystal clear river of life and the trees whose leaves are 'for the healing of the nations' (see Revelation 22:1–5).

Death and the early church

In the first few Christian centuries, martyrdom was the expected end for the most fervent believers. Stephen was the first martyr, and his death was seen as a model for much later Christian experience, expectation and endurance. During his trial, it was recorded that his accusers 'saw that his face was like the face of an angel' (Acts 6:15). A little while later, Luke records

> But Stephen, full of the Holy Spirit, looked up to heaven and saw the glory of God, and Jesus standing at the right hand of God. 'Look,' he said, 'I see heaven open and the Son of Man standing at the right hand of God.' (Acts 7:55–56)

Just over a century later, probably in AD 155, Polycarp, Bishop of Smyrna, was martyred. He was one of the most famous of his generation of Christians, a venerable old man who said he had 'served the Lord for 86 years'. He also taught Irenaeus of Lyons, who was one of the most attractive theologians and leaders of the next generation. The accounts of Polycarp's martyrdom[1] are widely accepted as authentic. Irenaeus tells us that the youthful Polycarp had been 'instructed by the Apostles, and had familiar intercourse with many who had seen Christ'.

The account of his martyrdom is deeply moving. The old man had foreseen it in an earlier vision. He faced his ordeal before the Roman Governor, and a howling mob, with immense courage. He prayed to the 'God of angels and powers', and refused to be nailed to the stake, saying, 'Let me be; He who gives me strength to endure the flames will give strength not to flinch at the stake, without you making sure of it with nails.' When he finished a lengthy prayer with a triumphant, 'Amen', the men set light to the fire. The eye-witness continues:

> And then we who were privileged to witness it saw a wondrous sight; and we have been spared to tell it to the rest of you. The fire took on the shape of a hollow chamber, like a ship's sail when the wind fills it, and formed a wall round about the martyr, and there was he in the centre of it, not like a human being in flames, but like a loaf baking in the oven, or like a gold or silver ingot being refined in the furnace. And we became aware of a delicious fragrance like the odour of incense.

Polycarp was eventually stabbed to death, and his body was retained by the authorities 'in case they should forsake the Crucified and take to worshipping this fellow instead'.

We also have detailed testimonies about 'after death' experiences from the writings about Martin of Tours, Augustine of Hippo and the Venerable Bede[2].

Modern experiences

Moving much closer to modern times, we consider stories from London, New Zealand and Nigeria.

In February 1911, Dorothy Kerin[3] aged twenty-two, was blind and apparently dying. Her well-documented illness had been diagnosed as an advanced state of tuberculosis and diabetes. She was in great pain, and very emaciated through lack of food.

Such was her condition, and now the end had come. About half-past nine on Sunday evening, as mother and friends stood watching, she seemed to breathe her last. Anyhow, for eight minutes her lungs ceased to breathe, and her heart ceased to beat, and they deemed her dead. But just at this juncture, Dorothy tells us someone called her by name, three times distinctly, and she replied, 'Yes, I am listening, who is it?' and he said, 'Listen!' and she felt two warm hands take hold of hers. A beautiful Light then flashed over the screen and came right over the bed. In the midst of the Light stood the Angel of the Lord, who, still holding her hands in his and lifting up to her eyes, and touching her ears, said 'Dorothy, your sufferings are over, get up and walk.'

She then opened her eyes and sat up, greatly wondering to see so many friends around her bed, to whom she said, 'I am well now! I want my dressing-gown. I want to walk.' Of course, her request was unheeded, and she began to get up without it, when her mother came and held her down, saying, 'No, Dorothy, you will fall, you must not get up!' While thus held, the angel again the second time said, 'Get up and walk!' Dorothy then appealed to her mother asking her if she did not hear, on which she then relaxed her hold on her, and someone suggested that the dressing-gown should be given her just to gratify her, and convince her that she could not walk.

Just then a part of the beautiful Light, seen only by Dorothy, came and stood at the right-hand side of her bed. Then, with eyes and ears opened, and strength imparted to every limb, she threw off the bedclothes from her, and stepped on to the floor, placing her hand upon the Light that was to lead her.

The Light then led her into another room, where she found her stepfather, and in the joy of her restoration she threw her arms around his neck and kissed him.

The Light then led her back again to her own room, where she found the whole company shaking and trembling with fear! Her stepfather, who was following her, then fell upon the floor, and began to cry – in the attitude of prayer.

The account concludes with Dorothy's request for a full meal (which is remarkably similar to Jesus' instructions to Jairus to give his daughter a meal, see Mark 5:43), and the general amazement and awe of all her friends. She had a perfect night's sleep, and the doctor, who had been expecting a request for a death certificate, was completely amazed. He kept saying, 'What does it all mean?'

For Dorothy, the meaning became quite clear. After many years of preparation and spiritual battles, she was able to open the famous house of healing at Burrswood, in Kent. When God grants such experiences, he expects people to put them to good effect!

A glimpse of eternity

Ian McCormack's story is, by any standard, remarkable[4]. Ian's testimony begins with his disillusionment at his confirmation service in New Zealand in the 1970s. At the age of fourteen, he expected to hear God speak to him. He embarrassed his father, his parish priest and his mother with his questions. He walked away, announcing that he would never come back to church. As he stamped off to the family car, his mother, uncharacteristically, yelled at him, 'Son, if I can teach you nothing else – remember one thing – however far you find yourself from God, if you cry to God from your heart, he will hear you and forgive you.'

For over ten years, Ian lived a carefree life. He sought pleasure in sport, travelling, surfing, and especially in scuba diving. Visiting the island of Mauritius in 1982, he enjoyed some magnificent scuba diving, catching huge lobsters, avoiding sharks...

All went well until one night when his torch picked up an interesting looking box-shaped jellyfish. He squeezed it with his leather gloves. Unlike the others in his party, he wasn't fully protected, and in return for his inquisitiveness, he received four stings from the deadliest jellyfish known to humanity – known as 'the invisible one' to the locals. One sting can kill a man in ten minutes.

By the time a terrified teenager got him to the shore, he was already paralysed on one side. The boy panicked and left him. He crawled into the middle of a road at 11 p.m. without much prospect of a rescue. The poison made him sleepy. He heard a voice saying, 'Son, if you close your eyes you will never awake again.' Moments later he crawled around a bend and found three taxi drivers. He heard the voice say, 'Son, are you willing to beg for your life?' Ian begged the taxi drivers to rescue him and to trust him to pay them later. Two laughed and walked away, the third agreed (with the promise of $50) to drive him to hospital. The third driver took him to a tourist hotel, decided that he would never pay his fare, and physically pushed him out of the taxi.

At the hotel he met a friend, Daniel, who couldn't believe that he'd been stung by 'the invisible' and wasn't yet dead. Three Chinese proprietors of the hotel wouldn't take him to hospital. He could feel the coldness of death creeping up his body; he knew enough veterinary science to know exactly what was happening to him.

Eventually, an ambulance arrived, because his Creole friend Daniel had phoned the hospital. On the way to the hospital his whole life flashed before him. He knew that he was going to die. Then he saw his mother, in a clear vision, praying for him in the ambulance... she began to share the same words with him that she had spoken after his confirmation. He didn't know which God to pray to, but decided that as his mother would pray to Jesus he'd better try that. He tried to remember the Lord's Prayer. In a jumbled fashion, it came back to him: 'Forgive us our sins.' Ian tried to list his sins, but settled for admitting his hypocrisy, particularly his desperation in turning to God at such a time. The next phrase that came to him was, 'Forgive those who have sinned against you.' He didn't feel there were many people that he needed to forgive.

Then he saw the face of the Indian taxi driver who had pushed him out of the car. 'Will you forgive him?' 'I wasn't planning to!' Then he saw the Chinese who had refused to take him to hospital. 'Will you forgive him?' Suddenly he realized that, to use a New Zealand expression, this was where 'the rubber meets the road'. Either he forgave these people, or he couldn't be forgiven. He prayed, 'If you can forgive me, I will forgive them.' The third phrase of the Lord's Prayer that he remembered was 'Thy will be done, on earth as it is in heaven.' He submitted to God's will, admitted that he'd been rebellious and wrong for twenty-six years, and promised to follow God for the rest of his life. He then remembered the whole prayer, and received a great sense of peace.

After arriving at the hospital, every emergency treatment was tried – without success. After about ten minutes, a doctor said kindly, but clearly, 'Son, I'm afraid we've done all we can for you.'

His eyes closed, he gave a great sigh of relief, and he found himself wide awake in a pitch black void. He had a huge sense of terror; he realized that he was 'out of his body', yet conscious. He said, 'Where am I?' Two voices spoke in the darkness. The first said, 'Shut up,' and the second, 'You deserve to be here, shut up.' Then one of the voices said, 'You're in hell – shut up!' and Ian heard the voice that he had heard when lying on the road saying, 'If you hadn't prayed that death-bed prayer in the ambulance that's where you would have stayed.'

Then he saw a brilliant light, and he was lifted up into the presence of an incredibly brilliant, but distant light. Waves came from the brightest source and filled his body with warmth, comfort, peace and joy. He was drawn closer to the source of the light which was as radiant as a mountain of diamonds. He wasn't sure whether the source was personal or impersonal.

Then the voice spoke again, 'Ian, if you return, you must

see in a new light.' He remembered words on a Christmas card that he had received, 'God is light; in him there is no darkness at all'. (He didn't know that this was a biblical text – 1 John 1:5.)

Ian felt completely unworthy, but wave after wave of light touched him, filling him with love and more love. Weeping, he cried out, 'I want to see you.' He felt a great healing radiance, and saw a man's feet, but where the face should have been there was a brilliant, dazzling light. (Afterwards Ian read Revelation 1:13–18 and recognized what he had seen as corresponding to the vision of John.) He was able to see behind the form of Jesus, and was shown a vision of Paradise, with green pastures, mountains, blue sky, trees and a crystal clear stream (again, afterwards, Ian read Revelation chapter 22 and 2 Peter 3:10–13 and recognized much of what he had seen). He remembered that he had travelled the world looking for such a place, and asked, 'Why wasn't I born here?' The voice replied, 'You've got to be born again, Ian, now that you've seen, do you want to step in or return?'

He wanted to say goodbye to the sick, tired world. No one would miss him. He had no debts. Then he remembered his mother. If he entered Paradise, she would assume that her prayers had been unanswered, and that he had entered a lost eternity. He saw that Jesus was the door to Paradise, leading on to green pastures (again, afterwards, he read John 10:7–9). He knew that he must speak to others to give them the same chance that he had been given, and he chose to go back.

The voice said, 'Tilt your head', and he woke up to see a terrified Indian doctor who was prodding his feet. He tilted his head the other way and saw the look of blank horror on the faces of the nurses and orderlies in the doorway of the room where he had been laid out – apparently dead for fifteen minutes.

For a moment he thought he had returned as a quadriplegic. He prayed, 'Lord, if you can't heal me...' Ian then felt an extraordinary warmth which lasted four hours, then he knew that he was completely healed. He walked out of the hospital the next day. None of the locals could face him. They thought he was a spirit who had returned, and they were terrified of him (a reaction not unlike those who prayed for Peter's release from prison!).

Ian, in his account, says quite humbly that he believes he 'died', but that others may prefer to interpret his experience in line with Paul's vision recorded in 2 Corinthians 12:2–4 where Paul writes with tantalizing brevity about an 'out-of-body' experience in Paradise.

Perhaps the most amazing part of his testimony was the experience of his mother, who, exactly when this drama was happening, woke up hearing a voice, 'Your son is nearly dead – pray for him.' Ian McCormack is not the first person, nor the last, to owe his salvation, humanly, to a godly, praying mother!

A Nigerian pastor

On Easter Day 2002, I watched a video clip of an account of a Nigerian pastor[5] who had suffered, in the previous November, an apparently fatal car accident. His wife had taken him to a hospital in Ouitsa, where he was in a critical condition. He had woken up, and commanded his wife to remove him to the hospital near his home in Owerri.

Against all medical advice, she obeyed. During the journey, he told her how to carry on his ministry, and care for their children, and then appeared to die.

On his arrival at Owerri, he was given a thorough examination by a doctor, pronounced dead, and placed in the mortuary. Both the doctor and the mortuary attendant testified in the video that he was dead. The doctor said, 'No breathing, no heartbeat, no pulse…'

On the third day after his arrival in Owerri, the German evangelist, Reinhard Bonnke, was opening a new church. A huge congregation had gathered. The pastor's wife believed that God had promised to raise her husband. In particular, she had received the text 'Women received back their dead, raised to life again' (Hebrews 11:35a). She, and the pastor's father, took his corpse out of the mortuary and went to the new church. She believed that the anointing at Bonnke's meeting would be such that a miracle would be possible.

Her amazing faith and courage were rewarded! When they arrived, the evangelist was preaching. The body was laid out in a side room. After the sermon, Bonnke started to pray for the sick. About that time, those watching the pastor's body saw that it had started to breathe. They told the church congregation, adding that his body was still stiff and frozen. At this stage, a crowd gathered to pray and praise God.

Someone had brought a video camera to the meeting (not unusual in Africa) and started to film what was happening. Gradually, life returned. For a while, one of the watchers massaged the pastor's neck. Suddenly he stood up. He immediately demanded to know, 'Where is my file?'

Gradually he explained that he had a vision of the next world. As he was dying, during the car journey to Owerri, he had been aware of two angels. They allowed him to give his

wife instructions about his house, his children and his congregation, but not to reveal their presence. He was given a
file in which to record his experiences. He was then taken
on a journey to a celestial city, which was far too beautiful
to describe (see 2 Corinthians 12:2–4). He had then been
given a glimpse of hell. Here, a pastor who had been a habit-
ual thief hailed him and told him to report that the 'prayer
of the rich man had been granted'. He noted this in his file,
but was puzzled as to what it meant.

In passing, we might remember that John was puzzled by
part of his vision and reduced to tears (see Revelation 5:4).

Later he realized that the strange reference to the rich
man referred to Luke 16:19–31, where the rich man asks
Abraham to send Lazarus to warn his brothers of their need
to repent. He believed that he had been sent back to give
this generation a final warning.

This extraordinary story was told with remarkable
restraint, and considerable corroboration from the doctor,
the mortuary attendant and those who saw the pastor come
back to life.

A Tanzanian newspaper covering Bonnke's crusade in
Arusha in July 2002 remarked with biting cynicism, 'How
come that there was a video camera available?' There is, however, no way that the film could have been faked; the actual
video evidence came near the end of the story, and anyone
who travels in Africa knows that in the more wealthy parts
of Africa, electronic equipment is quite common.

In the television programme, Bonnke is very careful to
disclaim any involvement in the miracle. He sees the event
as a very powerful sign to an unbelieving world performed
by a sovereign act of God in response to the faithful prayer
and action of the pastor's wife.

Three short accounts

We continue this chapter with three much shorter stories. The Dean of Chester Cathedral, Dr Gordon McPhate, interviewed in the *Church Times* in October 2002 tells how, at the age of eighteen, he was already intent on a medical career. He then talked about the event that took him beyond the limits of scientific understanding.

> I was in a car crash, and had an out-of-body experience during a cardiac arrest. It was only when I read the prologue from St John's Gospel in the Gideon Bible at my hospital bedside that I properly understood what had happened to me. Science alone could not make sense of my being outside my body, watching my self being resuscitated by paramedics. While outside my body, I had an encounter with a person. It was so loving that I did not want to leave. But somehow, it was communicated that I was to come back to fulfil a purpose. I still don't know fully what that purpose is. It unfolds as I go along.

So far, it has meant a life devoted to academic medicine, and ordination – quite an unusual combination! Dr McPhate's experience was certainly unexpected, and theologically transforming.

My second story was told to me by a distinguished Catholic lady, with whom I have often stayed in the South of France. It concerned a man whose wife had left him to set up home with his best friend. In despair, he attempted to hang himself. He was surprised to find himself on his bed, some distance from the rope, with his neck marked by the rope. He heard a voice saying, 'Don't do that again.' Not surprisingly, he became a believer, and is an active member of a prayer group in the region.

My third story comes from Dutch New Guinea. A friend, Priscilla, with whom I stayed in Argentina, told me about her childhood in what was then Dutch New Guinea (now Irian Jaya, although for political reasons its name keeps changing). Her father had had a dramatic conversion after fighting for the Germans in the war. He became a missionary, and landed by plane with a friend, in a remote area. The local tribesmen were quite welcoming and the two missionaries worked at literacy and spoke about Jesus. Priscilla who was born there says they witnessed every New Testament miracle in their time there.

Two things, in particular, stand out. As some of the village elders and others became Christians, they had a simple uncomplicated faith. One day, one of their leaders died. The others, following the example of Jesus, gathered around him and prayed for his recovery. When this took place, they told the missionaries who were of course overjoyed and very excited. The locals just remarked 'Why are you so surprised – it's in your book?' There are no accounts of the dead man having had visions of the next world, but the elders did mention that before the missionaries arrived two of them had a dream that white men would come out of the sky and show them how to find the true God. This certainly meant that the incoming missionaries were protected from serious harm in an area that certainly practised cannibalism.

Conclusions

The experiences cited in this chapter are by any yardstick unusual. Many different conclusions might be drawn. One serious researcher, Dr Maurice Rawlings, a cardiologist[6], was so shaken by some of his patients' accounts of 'out-of-body', and 'near-death' experiences, that he conducted serious research, both into people's experiences and into the teaching of the major religions about the afterlife. This was his conclusion:

> After a laborious study of comparative theology in the sacred books of many religions, including the Torah and Talmud of Judaism; the Koran; the Vedas, Upanishads, Brahmanas of Hinduism; the Avesta of Zoroastrianism; the sayings of Confucius; the Agamas of Jainism; the Tripitake of Buddhism; the Kojiki of Shintoism; the Tao-te-ching of Taoism; and the Analects, I have discovered that the one book that is the most descriptive of the after-death experiences of resuscitated patients is the Christian Bible.

He was also increasingly concerned by the 'bright light' phenomena which suggests that 'all would be well' in the afterlife – irrespective of previous lifestyle. One of his most seminal experiences was when he talked to a young man, aged twenty-one, who was recovering from three serious gunshot wounds.

His patient told him that he had an out-of-body experience, and had felt surrounded by a heavenly light which was 'understanding'. He felt no rejection. There was no examination of his past life. 'Peace and Love' were communicated. The young man was surprised, and told the doctor of his past life. It was not a pleasant tale – involving a double murder during a robbery three years earlier, and a dance in a bar with a 'woman' who turned out to be a cross-dressing homosexual man. He attacked his dance partner, and for his pains, he got shot three times in the chest.

Not surprisingly, he felt his experience of the accepting light was distinctly odd. He concluded by asking a question, 'Doc, does God ever make mistakes?' Dr Rawlings concluded that this was a clear example of Satan masquerading as an 'angel of light'. Ian McCormack agrees. One questioner asked him how he accounted for near-death experiences where people experienced neither hell nor Jesus. He replied robustly that these experiences were deceptions because the true God requires repentance. Certainly, experiences of the 'all will be well' type, and which lead to no discernible change of lifestyle or belief, would seem to be misleading.

Dr Alison Morgan, in her powerful book, *What Happens When We Die?* looked at various hypotheses about these experiences. She writes[7]:

Are there any natural explanations of the near-death experience? Most researchers into the near-death experience have not limited themselves to the mere collecting of data. They have sought in a great variety of ways to find a hypothesis which would explain those data, and all kinds of theories have been put forward to explain the NDE in purely naturalistic terms. Such theories fall into three groups.

1. The NDE is caused by medical or physiological factors such as oxygen deprivation, the effect of pain-killing or other drugs, the malfunctioning of the central nervous system, fever and biochemical reactions in the brain.
2. The NDE is caused by psychological factors such as unconscious wishful thinking, hallucination and self-protective devices.
3. The NDE is caused by religious or cultural factors; people experience what they expect to experience.

The problem with these hypotheses is that none of them successfully accounts for all the documented instances of the near-death experience; examples can be found to disprove each one. The findings of parapsychologists Karlis Osis and Erlendur Haraldsson are particularly important in this regard. Osis and Haraldsson sent questionnaires on the experiences of the dying to over 2,000 doctors and nurses in both America and India, and conducted a detailed computer analysis of the returns. They found that there was no correlation whatsoever between medical, psychological or religious factors and the occurrence or nature of a near-death experience. So, for example, patients treated with sedatives or drugs, and those suffering from illnesses normally associated with the presence of hallucinations were in fact less likely, not more likely, to have an NDE than other patients. And those who hallucinated while suffering from a particular medical condition reported seeing living persons, whereas near-death visions were invariably of deceased persons. Oxygen deprivation, stress, expectations of death or recovery, the presence of particular

psychological states, adherence to Christianity or
Hinduism and other possible factors appear to have had
no influence on either the occurrence or the non-occur-
rence of the NDE. The researchers were forced to conclude that there is no naturalistic explanation currently
available to us which can account satisfactorily for the
near-death experience.

We should not draw too many conclusions from the small
number of stories that I have cited. However, it is worth not-
ing that in almost every case, the survivors were surprised
by their theological discoveries, and led fruitful Christian
lives as a result.

Dorothy Kerin had been unwell for many years, probably since the death of her father when she was only twelve.
Brought up in a Christian home, her vision and healing led
to a lifetime of service. By contrast, Ian McCormack had no
expectation of a future life, and was very startled by his
encounters – experiencing both a little of the terrors of eternal darkness, and a great deal of the light of Christ and the
beauty of Paradise. He has used his new life to bear witness
to the saving power of Jesus, and to warn people of the dangers of living as he had done previously. The Nigerian pastor's vision of the future life was very much in accordance
with what he already believed, though obviously he and all
those who witnessed it were given a much greater urgency
to proclaim the full message of the gospel.

In every case, the fruits of these experiences were beneficial, both to the individuals and to those around them. We
cannot build a theology from anecdotes, however powerful.
But each story does bear witness to the power of the risen
Lord, the place of angels in the world to come and the

dangers of impenitence, and for these reasons I am happy to include them, even if they do not fit into a neat, tidy theological package.

Notes

1. Penguin Classics, *Early Christian Writings*, 1968, pp. 153ff.
2. See John Woolmer, *Angels*, Oxford: Monarch, 2003, pp. 167–175.
3. Dorothy Arnold, Dorothy Kerin, *Called by Christ to Heal*, London: Hodder & Stoughton, 1965, p. 9.
4. Ian McCormack, *A Glimpse of Eternity*, Kingdom Power Trust Video, from St Andrew's Church, Chorleywood.
5. Broadcast on Cable TV, 21 March 2002, interview with Reinhard Bonnke.
6. Maurice Rawlings, M.D., *To Hell and Back*, Nashville: Nelson, 1993.
7. Dr Alison Morgan, *What Happens When We Die?*, Eastbourne: Kingsway, 1995, pp. 80–81.

CHAPTER 8

Angels and Psychic Experiences

ANGELS ARE NEWSWORTHY. Many books have been published, and some TV programmes devoted to a fairly uncritical study of people's experiences. A typical example was the well-researched episode in the *Everyman* series, put out on BBC 1 early in the year 2000. Most of the programme was based on the careful research of a young PhD student called Emma Heathcote-James.

Very wisely, she neither put forward her own views, nor much analysis of people's experiences. She was clearly moved by people's stories, and accepted that, in most cases, something strange had happened to them. She had received over 600 stories. They came from a wide range of faiths, and included some from agnostics and atheists. All believed that they, or their relatives had seen, and been helped by, angels. The majority of the stories did not come from practising Christians. However, a number of those who were featured in the programme had been encouraged by Christians (or at least by those with Christian sympathies).

One of the most powerful stories was shared by a blind lady who told of a tearful journey by train from Birmingham to London, shortly after her father's death. She spoke of having a vision of angels taking her father to heaven. The angels (as in Luke 15:10) were rejoicing. To her, what was particularly beautiful, as one blind from birth, was that she was able to see the angels, and to understand what joy looked like.

Many of the other experiences were similar to ones that I have recorded – a man being rescued from probable death when surfing; a woman moved out of the way when a car was about to crash into the wall by her shop where she was standing; a man being comforted by an angel in hospital after a severe illness and people seeing angels just before a close relative died.

Another interesting story was provided by a woman whose father had told her about his sight of the Angel of Mons during the First World War (see also Chapter 6). Her father had won the Military Cross, but like many others who survived the horrors of the trenches, declined to speak about his heroics.

He did tell his daughter about the time that the Allies were facing a complete rout at Mons. They had already lost nearly half of an army of 60,000, mainly because of superior German firepower. He and his comrades were amazed to see the enemy suddenly turn round and flee. They looked up, and saw the white cavalry in the sky. His reaction, after the war, was to tell his family always to trust Jesus Christ who had delivered the British army from certain defeat.

He also commented that many people saw the angels, some of whom were religious adherents, some not. Not all the information came from the British side. Dr Moolenburgh[1] records receiving a letter from a German woman who had been an intelligence officer in the Luftwaffe in the Second World War. Her father had told her how he and other German soldiers had been temporarily blinded by angels at Yprès, in the First World War.

All of these examples clearly helped people, and

strengthened their faith in God, and in many cases pointed them towards Jesus. Intermingled with these testimonies were a number of examples from people whom I would call professional angel watchers.

These people, who appeared to have various psychic properties, saw angels everywhere – one woman claimed to be able to travel on a bus and sense that it was completely overcrowded, because most of the passengers had angels attached to them. Others appeared to be making a living from selling angel clothes and trinkets, while others were encouraging people on psychic journeys where they would be able to visualize their angels. 'I can bring people in touch with their angels', was a fairly typical claim.

The programme included comments by a psychologist who made a number of carefully scripted negative comments. 'Fashions come and go – today it is angels, a few years ago it was out-of-body experiences.' 'Such experiences are always accompanied with a sense of very bright light – a hyperactive force in the visual cortex.' 'Stress and fear induce these sorts of experiences.'

By contrast, the young researcher, who was obviously surprised by the results of her research, remarked that in her experience only about 20 percent of the testimonies were in stress-related situations.

The overall impression is, inevitably, of spiritual confusion – a tangled web of experiences with very little available criteria with which to sort the wheat from the chaff. What is the source of this confusion? *Aren't all angel experiences good?*

Source of confusion (1):
Literature about angels and spirit guides

Books about angels tend to fall into one of two categories – the majority, which are often found on the shelves of high street shops or in the specialist shops of places like Glastonbury, are largely uncritical. Angels are to be welcomed, stories shared and the spiritual world is there to be contacted. A minority, usually written from a biblical standpoint, are very critical and full of warnings about deception. In this chapter, we will look at the different viewpoints. It is an important matter about which we need to know the truth.

Can angels really deceive us?
Many books can be found which purport to teach us how to get in touch with angels, how to receive healing from angels, how angelic hierarchies work and so on. Such books often contain a few references to the Bible, while confidently proclaiming that the writer knows better than Scripture on a wide variety of subjects. Numerous testimonies of angelic help, many of which are likely to be genuine, are included. What are we make of all of this?

Some New Age books have a considerable veneer of Christian teaching. This, in my view, makes them from a Christian perspective, even more dangerous. An interesting example is called *Spirit Guides and Angel Guardians*[2]. The author quotes various Christian texts about guidance (e.g. Isaiah 65:24 and Philippians 4:13). He even gives the classic Colossian warning (Colossians 2:18) about not worshipping angels, and tells the story of angel choirs singing near Lee Abbey[3].

The opening chapters are quite scriptural. However, by page 27, things are beginning to change. Lucifer (Satan) is seen as responding to God's request for 'a volunteer to go to Earth to help mankind'. The storytellers (the biblical writers) gradually forgot that 'Lucifer was sent down by God to test humankind. Instead, he became regarded as a force for evil'. By the middle of the book we have an extraordinary mishmash including a 'quotation' from Augustine of Hippo, enthusiasm for Native American Chiefs, Chinese sages and Egyptian priests who 'guide' spiritualist mediums. There is also an amazing statement about the Ouija board which 'can be a useful instrument when used responsibly'. After a brief warning about the possibility of encountering 'negative spirits', there is a powerful biblical quotation:

> Dear friends, do not believe every spirit, but test the spirits to see whether they are from God, because many false prophets have gone out into the world. This is how you can recognise the Spirit of God: Every spirit that acknowledges that Jesus Christ has come in the flesh is from God, but every spirit that does not acknowledge Jesus is not from God. This is the spirit of the antichrist, which you have heard is coming and even now is already in the world. (1 John 4:1–3)

The apostle John would be astonished to find his trenchant spiritual test misused as a user-friendly text to justify spirit guides and the use of the Ouija board (it is perhaps typical of the age we live in that one of the most successful racehorses of 2004 was called Ouija Board)!

Another typical example of one of these sort of books (*Angels and Companions in Spirit*[4]) has a chapter answering people's questions. In the midst of this we find the following: 'In the Universe we never die'; 'human beings have fashioned the devil... in order to avoid taking responsibility for their own malicious attitudes and destructive behaviour; 'Smoke only when the spirits tell you to' (Angelica as used by Californian Indians, cannabis and varieties of mushrooms are amongst other things recommended). 'The misuse of spirit guide information generates terrifying karma.' 'As a practising Quaker, I can report that my years of experience with spirit guide work have only served to deepen my faith. Many Saints and Biblical figures have sought and received the advice of angels. The Laws in Deuteronomy and Leviticus have since been rephrased in the New Testament, or modified by Christian authorities and proponents of Reformed Judaism, or abandoned entirely.'

All of which is pretty remarkable! Anyone who takes the Bible seriously will quickly discover that there is no divergence between the Old and New Testament:

> Let no one be found among you... who practices divination or sorcery, interprets omens, engages in witchcraft, or casts spells, or who is a medium or spiritist or who consults the dead. (Deuteronomy 18:10–11)

> A number who had practiced sorcery brought their scrolls together and burned them publicly. (Acts 19:19)

These are just two of many texts which warn everyone to steer well clear of things that are spiritually dangerous[5].

Another popular book, *Sylvia Browne's Book of Angels*[6] tells very persuasively of the author's psychic experiences. She describes how her 'gifts' were inherited from her grandmother. She quotes from the Bible and the religious texts of other faiths. She is convinced that nowadays many people are having genuine experiences of angels and gives this interesting reason: 'I think the sudden resurgence of angels is also in direct rebuttal to the hellfire and demons we've had to put up with from so many religions' (page 29).

She tells how she founded a Gnostic Church called the Society of Novus Spiritus descended from Essenes, Knight's Templar and Cathars and claims that 'we are the oldest religion – the religion practiced by Christ'. She is scathing of biblical Christianity, writing (page 46):

> Contrary to popular belief, there are no dark angels. Some religious texts warn us to be careful of 'evil angels'. Others say that Satan is a fallen angel. Not only is there no Devil, but Raheim [one of her spirit guides – apparently last seen on earth as a Sikh teacher of renown] says 'I have never seen a dark angel, ever. There are no evil angels and there are no dark or fallen angels'.

Later on (page 175) she answers the question: Is Satan a fallen angel?

> Logically, why should there just be one entity with a horn and a tail? Satan is not just one single being, but a group of entities separated from God in the beginning... This earth plane is the only hell we will endure, and this is where the dark entities seem to survive; but with God's army of angels, spirit guides, the Holy Spirit, and the Christ consciousness, white entities will always overcome evil, even if at times they seem to be losing. Ultimately, what goes around comes around.

The author and her spirit guide Raheim clearly think that they know better than Jesus who spent a lot of his time exorcising demons and teaching in his parables about 'the devil and his angels' (see Matthew 25:41). She also writes that:

> I find it a little inaccurate to say that only one angel such as Gabriel addressed Mary and told her she was carrying the Christ child. No, Mary was visited by many angels...

Such 'knowledge' is presumably acquired from her spirit guides who also teach her in detail about ten orders of angels (angels, archangels, cherubim, seraphim, powers, carrions, virtues, dominions, thrones, principalities); most of these have a biblical origin although carrions certainly don't and virtues are found only in books claiming connection with the Bible but which were rightly not included in the canon of Scripture. The Bible gives no hierarchy and is pretty silent about their various duties. Our author produces this interesting statement about the virtues:

> Their primary purpose is to help us with our charts, those blue prints for our life here on earth that we create on the Other Side before we are born into an incarnation... In our charts, we choose the time of our birth, our zodiac sign, our parents, our children and friends, our location on this earth... (page 129)

This remarkable statement is plainly ridiculous. How can we choose both our parents and our children? What about their choice? Psalm 139 puts matters profoundly and very differently:

For you created my inmost being; you knit me together
in my mother's womb. I praise you because I am fear-
fully and wonderfully made; your works are wonderful, I
know that full well. My frame was not hidden from you
when I was made in the secret place. When I was woven
together in the depths of the earth, your eyes saw my
unformed body (Psalm 139:13–16).

Within the text of the book, there are surprisingly few actual
angel stories. Most of them are about escape from and
avoidance of traffic accidents. They may well be true
accounts, but they are all fairly insignificant events and
none of them support the extraordinary theories of the
book. She answers various questions including 'What is the
difference between spirit guides and angels?'

Angels were made as companions and protectors to
humanity. Spirit guides, on the other hand, have lived
lives in order to perfect. The chance that we will be or
have been a spirit guide is 100 percent.

There is of course the usual reincarnation myth and a
denial of any sort of judgment.

We decide what we want to review (of our life after
death) and at what pace we want to review it. The choice
is entirely up to us, and we're the ones who judge our
lives. Contrary to popular belief, no one on the Other
Side judges us. We're the ones who applaud or abrade
ourselves, if we so choose.

Another assertion of breathtaking self-confidence! Perhaps this is the moment to tackle the issue of reincarnation on which much of this spiritual edifice depends.

The deception of reincarnation

It is easy to see why people chase after such experiences. In today's lonely, frenetic world many churches seem unfriendly, and unspiritual. By contrast, many New Age people are warm, welcoming, concerned about the environment, and very willing to help one another. Besides all this, there is the ultimate problem of death. Reincarnation points to a nice hopeful solution. It deals with failure, and offers peace and reassurance.

The trouble is that it is completely wrong! Wrong, because it undermines the cross of Christ: 'You [an individual, unique person] were bought at a price. Therefore honour God with your body' (1 Corinthians 6:20). Wrong, because there is no evidence for it. It is quite extraordinary how people's pre-incarnations are usually of famous people; and how intertwined and complicated 'relationships' become. Wrong, because humankind isn't getting any better. If reincarnation were true, there would be clear evidence of progress in our attitudes, lifestyle, relationships. Wrong, because it is mathematically impossible.

A typical statement about reincarnation reads 'I have had 30,000 previous incarnations'. A statement that you never find in these books is 'I am a first-time incarnate soul'. Curious, because mathematically it is quite impossible for all of us to be reincarnations of other humans – unless, of course, you believe in souls on other planets, etc!

It is sometimes alleged that the Bible teaches reincarnation (the appearance of Moses and Elijah on the Mount of Transfiguration is cited, particularly with reference to Matthew 17:12, which is interpreted to identify John the Baptist with Elijah). Also it is suggested that Jesus taught reincarnation. On the contrary, his teaching on the importance of each individual could hardly be clearer. Jesus makes this particularly clear in the parable of the lost sheep – which is preceded by one of the classic guardian angels texts:

> See that you do not look down on one of these little ones. For I tell you that their angels in heaven always see the face of my Father in heaven.
>
> What do you think? If a man owns a hundred sheep, and one of them wanders away, will he not leave the ninety-nine on the hills and go to look for the one that wandered off? And if he finds it, I tell you the truth, he is happier about that one sheep than about the ninety-nine that did not wander off. In the same way your Father in heaven *is not willing that any of these little ones should be lost*. (Matthew 18:10–14, my italics)

Healing with the Angels[7] is another book in much the same vein. It, too, depends on spirit guides who provide all sorts of extraordinary revelations and some pretty dull advice. There is only one account of healing (p. 32) in the whole book and it is nothing more than a recovery for a six-year-old in a hospital emergency aided and abetted by a deceased aunt and a deceased family friend. For the most part, the angels provide help with traffic problems, find lost property, guide about houses to buy... it is all very materialistic and rather reflects the spiritual culture of the Western world at this very materialistic time. On page 9 the angels write this to the readers:

> You like everyone else who is incarnated at this time, are a holy perfect child of God. We realize you may not always feel perfect and holy, and we also realize that you often don't act in that way. Nonetheless, God created your soul as a literal 'chip off the old block'. It contains God-essence, or Divine light, that can never be extinguished, soiled or taken away from you. Nothing you ever do would eradicate your Divine heritage.

Try telling the spiritual nonsense that every incarnated being is 'a perfect holy child of God' to the victims of Hitler, murderers or rapists. Try telling that spiritual nonsense to people who know that they are sinners and need God's forgiveness. Try telling that to the angels who witnessed the resurrection on the first Easter morning after the Son of God had suffered appallingly to bear the sins of a fallen world.

If these books are correct, then Christianity is a huge deception; but even if Christianity were proved to be false, I would suggest that their view of human nature is plainly false and that their teachings, albeit very well-meant, are based on dangerous spiritual experiences. Angel stories are one thing – teaching supposed to be given by spirit guides, angels or archangels from another world is quite another.

Source of confusion (2):
Encourage psychic experience and
develop your psychic gifting

Some years ago, a popular children's book called *The Dark is Rising* portrayed a new age when the ancient religions would flourish once again. In contrast, the church was portrayed as kindly, bumbling, out of touch and ineffectual.[8] Unfortunately, this is sometimes all too true!

All around the UK, especially around the ancient town of Glastonbury in Somerset, psychic activities flourish. Walk down Glastonbury high street, enjoy the scent of smoked grass, have your tarot reading, buy a crystal, have your allergy tested by a pendulum, buy books on angels, healings, numerology, clairvoyance, white witchcraft, Wicca... For the most part, it is all very amicable, very friendly; occasional conflicts break out with drunken wayfarers or destitute hippies, while kindly Christians in the parish church and other churches do their best to minister to people's spiritual and bodily needs. Here is a warning testimony.

A Glastonbury experience

Several years ago, I injured my neck following a road traffic accident and a judo injury. Despite seeing various GPs, physiotherapists and osteopaths, and taking various tablets, I was never free of pain. However, I endeavoured to keep fit and attended a leisure centre for several years. One day when talking to a gentleman, the conversation turned to my neck injury and the ongoing pain. He told me that he and his partner were healers in Glastonbury and offered his help. He gave me his card which read 'Healer and Counsellor', in case I wished to contact him. I said I would think about it.

Eventually, as the pain continued, I phoned and made an appointment. I went to see him weekly for over a year. I wasn't told what type of healing it was despite asking how it worked. Initially, we had a discussion to discover anything I needed to talk about and, on each occasion, I would open up to him. I would then lie on the couch and he would go round my body with his hands just over me. This generally took between one to two hours. I was asked to make a donation of whatever I could afford.

At this time I was involved in a relationship (not with the healer) which ended abruptly, and I found myself very low afterwards. The healer told me that healing would help, so I continued with it. I was given some 'sayings' to repeat morning and evening. I can't remember them, but I now realise that they encouraged me to isolate myself from others. At one point I asked if this was a religious healing group, but he merely laughed and said, 'I thought you would say that.'

Gradually, I began to develop an interest in psychic things and was encouraged to go to a spiritualist church. Whilst there, I asked two healers if they thought I could heal. They told me to open my hands, and then said there was something there. I was encouraged by the Glastonbury healer to read widely about healing and started to read any books relating to healing and psychic issues. I was also receiving psychic mail.

I began to have premonitions, which increased my anxiety. One related to the Paddington rail disaster. When I told the healer, he said that I was discovering my psychic powers and that he would teach me to 'cover up' and protect myself from this. He also said that being a nurse, I needed to protect myself when I went into the hospital by covering myself (mentally) with a white blanket. This was also important when treating patients. It took me nearly two years to move on and forget this strange idea.

During this time I went to France with my parents and son. I felt strange at times, with a sense of déjà vu. Once, on a beach, I saw a figure in white which, I believe, was an angel, spirit, or apparition. Strangely, when I got home I had a compulsion to search and read about Camille Monet (the wife of the Impressionist artist) who had died in her early thirties. When I told the healer, he said it was the work of the infinite spirit world.

I told my sister that I had psychic/healing powers and that various psychics had confirmed this ability. I tried to heal my sister, but she was angry with me and told me I needed psychiatric help.

About this time I also began to get blinding headaches, and became forgetful and often confused as to my whereabouts when shopping, particularly in the supermarket. My GP prescribed anti-depressants and anti-psychotics. I phoned the Glastonbury healer and said I couldn't go any more, and that my family didn't agree with what I was doing. He said this was absolute madness and he told me to phone him anytime, any day, if I wanted to go back.

I was very afraid that these people would use their powers in a telepathic form to encourage me to join them. I also felt that I had been taken over, or possessed by something, and that I was losing control of myself and this 'something' was taking over. I began to have severe panic attacks; my mother realized the danger and asked John Woolmer to see me. My doctor also encouraged the church to get involved. John and another senior member of the local church came to see me. They listened to my story, and prayed very gently. Afterwards I felt safe, and no longer afraid. I also felt that the dark presence had left.

My friend is not yet a worshipping Christian, but writes hoping that her words will help others avoid the same sort of mistake. Many books encourage their readers to experience and to pass on the sort of psychic healing that the story above warns against.

Obviously, it is possible for Christians to go to absurd lengths condemning all sorts of practices. For instance, herbal medicine is often beneficial. Many of our modern drugs are based on old herbal remedies. I well remember walking in a rainforest in Kenya with a guide, who pointed out the medicinal uses of many of the plants and trees. The problems arise when such medicines are 'prayed over' by people using 'psychic powers'.

A hundred years ago, practices like table turning, automatic writing, and even spiritualism were regarded as harmless occupations – particularly for the leisured classes. My aunt who lived to a great age, and who died in 1988, told me of one such experience. She was the very essence of a respectable, God-fearing, 'Victorian' lady – someone of considerable spiritual understanding and grace.

In about 1919, she went to play tennis at a famous house in Yorkshire called Burton Agnes. The house was known to be haunted. There was an old legend concerning a skull that resided on the drawing room mantelpiece. A new owner removed it, placing it behind a wall. It 'screamed', until returned to its rightful place. Be that as it may, it was certainly a house which generated psychic presence and power (see, perhaps, Luke 5:17 for the Christian equivalent). The weather was terrible, tennis was impossible.

The party tried 'table turning' (an attempt to contact the dead which was fashionable particularly after the First World War). Aunt Hilda was terrified that they would attempt to contact her beloved brother Jim, who had recently died of wounds sustained in the terrible battle of the Somme. However, soon after they had started, proceedings were abruptly terminated when, in my aunt's words: 'The table took off, crashed into a wall, and everyone was terrified.'

Interestingly, my godmother, from very much the same generation, was troubled by disturbing dreams, and in her nineties asked me to pray for peace and calm, which I think she received. Her family had been interested in table turning, and she certainly acknowledged both its dangers and its baleful effect.

Much of this seems harmless, but the effects are long-lasting. Nowadays the Ouija board, tarot cards, Shamanism and spirit guides are more in fashion. Modern writings often defend, indeed encourage such practices.

There are many warnings in Scripture about the 'signs' that Satan can perform.

The LORD said to Moses and Aaron, "When Pharaoh says to you, 'Perform a miracle,' then say to Aaron, 'Take your staff and throw it down before Pharaoh,' and it will become a snake." So Moses and Aaron went to Pharaoh and did just as the LORD commanded. Aaron threw his staff down in front of Pharaoh and his officials, and it became a snake. Pharaoh then summoned the wise men and sorcerers, and the Egyptian magicians also did the same things by their secret arts. Each one threw down his staff and it became a snake. But Aaron's staff swallowed up their staffs. Yet Pharaoh's heart became hard and he would not listen to them, just as the LORD had said. (Exodus 7:8–13)

For false Christs and false prophets will appear and perform signs and miracles to deceive the elect – if that were possible. So be on your guard; I have told you everything ahead of time. But in those days, following that distress, 'the sun will be darkened, and the moon will not give its light...' (Mark 13:22–24)

The coming of the lawless one will be in accordance with the work of Satan displayed in all kinds of counterfeit miracles, signs and wonders, and in every sort of evil that deceives those who are perishing. They perish because they refused to love the truth and so be saved. (2 Thessalonians 2:9–10)

And he performed great and miraculous signs, even causing fire to come down from heaven to earth in full view of men. Because of the signs he was given power to do on behalf of the first beast, he deceived the inhabitants of the earth. He ordered them to set up an image in honour of the beast... (Revelation 13:13–14a)

The key question is, what is the fruit of such 'signs'? Are the people who perform signs basing their lives upon the teachings of Jesus? Are their lives built on his words, and their deeds done in his name, and at the 'will of my Father who is in heaven'? (Matthew 7:21)

Elsewhere Jesus said, of the Holy Spirit,

> But when he, the Spirit of truth, comes, he will guide you into all truth. He will not speak on his own; he will speak only what he hears, and he will tell you what is yet to come. He will bring glory to me by taking from what is mine and making it known to you. (John 16:13–14)

True signs bring glory to Jesus. False signs bring glory (and often financial gain!) to humans.

Source of confusion (3):
Confuse the Christian church

This happens in many ways. Speculation about Jesus' return, a false use of spiritual gifts, false guidance and confusion about the existence of Satan are four of the most common.

Confusion about the second coming

In Mark 13:5, Jesus warns about deception concerning the second coming. False miracles (Mark 13:22 and 2 Thessalonians 2:9), and false dating of the second coming (unknown to the angels or to Jesus – Matthew 24:36) are particularly common errors. Dr Moolenburgh[9], who writes much on the subject of angels, is particularly strong on this point:

In January 1991, a strange story was told. A Dutchman, driving his car along the motorway, picked up a hitch-hiker. When the car was once again travelling at considerable speed, the hitchhiker suddenly started to warn the driver in a serious tone that Jesus was on the point of returning. The driver looked round at him rather pityingly, and realised, to his intense shock, that he was in the car alone. The hitchhiker seemed to have vanished into thin air. Badly frightened, he parked his car on the hard shoulder, where a traffic policeman soon stopped to ask him what he was doing there. The policeman then helped the man, who was in a fairly distraught condition.

The so-called 'Angel on the motorway' was a great success in evangelical circles. There was a great deal of speculation about it from every quarter. A vicar spoke on the subject from the pulpit, articles appeared in magazines, and even radio and TV stations devoted some time to it. A sergeant from the traffic police inserted a message in the police newspaper, asking the policeman concerned to come forward. The strange thing is that this story was not new. Although it was described as having 'just happened', the story was much older. In 1983, a similar rumour was circulating in Germany.

I, too, heard this sort of story back in the 1980s when there was a lot of hysteria about the date 1984. Moolenburgh calls this 'a monkey roll' story:

The stories have one other thing in common: they cannot be verified. Everyone who tells the story has heard it second hand. No one knows anyone who was directly

involved. This means that the whole affair can be cate-
gorised as what is known in my part of the Netherlands
as a 'monkey roll' story. In case the reader is not familiar
with this sort of story, here is an example. My aunt has a
cleaning lady whose niece told her that in Amsterdam
there's a butcher who sells rolls with monkey's meat. It
must be true, because the other day I heard it from a
man whose brother's wife had been told so herself by the
baker, whose eldest son had eaten a monkey roll.

Everyone believes the monkey roll story, but no one
knows exactly who was involved or where it took place.

He points out that the angel shouldn't have made the driver
commit a serious traffic offence (picking up a hitchhiker on
a motorway), the angel shouldn't have startled the driver by
disappearing, and shouldn't have claimed to have knowledge that it was impossible for an angel to have (Mark
13:32)! In other words, the story was a none-too-subtle
deception.

Far more blatant was the cult in Uganda which caused a
hysterical mass suicide (or, perhaps, murder) when the new
millennium didn't bring the return of Jesus. A pastor friend
of mine was the first Christian on the scene; he spoke mov-
ingly, to me, of the horror of arriving at the burning buildings. The cult leaders appear to have escaped, with
considerable proceeds, to nearby Congo. If this is true, the
deception was criminal rather than demonic. The result was
just as bad.

Spiritual gifts that confuse and mislead
Some years ago, we were concluding a Parish Weekend with
a time of ministry. A small team, unused to such matters,

prepared to pray for the Holy Spirit to bless individuals. We had just started to pray – there were about a dozen people present – when one lady started to sing. She was singing 'spiritual songs', but something seemed to be wrong. Paul may have had the grace to put up with this for several days, but I had had enough after a few minutes.

Quietly, but firmly, I told her to 'shut up in the name of the Lord'. Graciously, she left the room. Back home, she was released from an evil spirit connected with her religious background, and afterwards, I believe, grew strongly in the Lord. This became a particularly significant evening which resulted, amongst other things, in three people becoming involved in full-time Christian ministry. Satan, with subtle soothing singing, was trying to prevent such an outcome.

A much more significant example comes from the church in Finland, told to me by the Revd Dr Mark Stibbe.

Deception in Finland

One of the most disturbing and destructive cases of deception I've ever come across occurred in the late nineties in Scandinavia. It still pains me to write or speak about these events today.

One of the biggest charismatic churches in Northern Europe was split by a man who appeared to have been dramatically converted from a New Age background. We will call him Hans.

The senior pastor of the large church in question (let's call him Eric) had been praying for revival for a long time and felt that this was it. Certainly the stories of people being saved and healed were very dramatic. The numbers of those reported to be coming to faith were also very impressive. The fact that the new converts were from a New Age background also aroused interest. Furthermore, the person at the epicentre of this movement had an extraordinary ability to see into people's lives and to speak about hidden things.

Eric became intimately involved with the inner core of this group. However, over a period of time, disturbing views started to emerge. The leaders began to teach that the Bible was not necessary because you could receive revelation directly from the Father – revelation that was 100 percent accurate. This knowledge was received during trances, experienced by those who led the movement, especially by Hans.

Not surprisingly, having left Scripture behind, unbiblical practices started to appear. The most blatant of these was the view that men could have two wives – one by legal marriage and a 'soul wife' from within the movement. Needless to say, Eric's marriage subsequently broke up. This was tragic not only because of the dreadful unhappiness it caused to his wife and children; but also because Eric's wife who had also been converted out of a New Age background, had discerned all along that there were very mixed spirits at work here.

I was somewhat involved in the assessment of this situation. Initially, when I met Hans, I was ambivalent. On the one hand, he was clearly able to see things by virtue of some kind of supernatural insight. On the other, there was something in my spirit that was uneasy. While he was saying the right things doctrinally (at this stage), something did not ring true. Yet he was so credible and persuasive, I felt led to be generally positive. I did not see that he was possessed by a spirit of divination.

How easy it is to be deceived! Looking back on it, I can see the symptoms of deception and I shall be a lot more cautious next time the spectacular hits my radar. The effects of this movement have been devastating. Marriages have been wrecked, a church almost destroyed (though now, thankfully being restored), and the prophetic discredited in a whole nation. We should all be careful not to become complacent. If that senior pastor could be deceived, anyone can be.

False guidance and deceiving dreams

Cindy Jacobs[10] gives an enlightening example:

> One day a man called me and said that God had told him that his wife did not have a strong enough anointing to match the call on his life. He said, therefore, she was going to die and that God was going to give him another wife. Even more astounding was that he convinced his wife that this was true. Fortunately, he was open to instruction and soon saw the error of in his thinking.

Cindy Jacobs continues her book with a description of an encounter with a woman, who she calls Louise, who was involved in serious prayer intercession:

> Louise began talking excitedly about how God blesses mature prayer intercessors with special intimacy with him. The word intimacy triggered something inside me. A red flag went up. As I asked her to tell me more, she described how Jesus would come to her at night and take her into the bridal chamber. When she said 'Jesus would come in the night' three red flags went up.

When the whole story came out, it was apparent she
had been involved in grave deception. She was actually
being attacked by evil spirits. Ministry involved renunciation of the deceiving spirit, repentance for believing the
lie, investigation as to how Satan had got a foothold (in
this case a disappointing marriage), Biblical work on the
difference between spiritual joy and physical arousal,
and taking authority over the incubus spirit and telling it
never to return.

Cindy discovered that the problem occurred with some
other prayer leaders, particularly those with disappointing
marriages or who had suffered an early bereavement.
Common sense could have unmasked all these deceptions;
but common sense is a quality which quickly disappears in
the somewhat supercharged spiritual atmospherics!

Anthony, one of the greatest spiritual leaders of the third
century, had similar troubles in his hermitage[11].

Confusion about the existence and origin of Satan

New Age writers tend to deny that Satan is a fallen angel:
but many clergy go further and deny existence of the devil
and evil spirits.

Some years ago, I was invited to preach in a cathedral. A
member of the cathedral staff, a very interesting and compassionate theologian, had stated, publicly, that he didn't
believe in the devil. Perhaps foolishly, I decided to put forward a different viewpoint. The set readings for the service
included some instructions of Jesus to the disciples.

Calling the Twelve to him, he sent them out two by two
and gave them authority over evil spirits. (Mark 6:7)

I included various stories about the reality of evil powers, and of the interest of the public in white witchcraft and related matters – as illustrated by the shelves of major booksellers, and current articles in *The Times*.

The reaction to the sermon was interesting. Many people, including one senior clergyman, thanked me profusely, the theologian smiled quizzically, and one or two people pressed me on the details of some of the material that I had included. Some local pagans, justifiably upset by an anecdote that was unintentionally identifiable, demanded a 'pistols-at-dawn' confrontation. Honour was satisfied with a Channel 4 television programme called *The Good, the Bad and the Pagans*. The 'good', I suppose, were represented by myself and a young woman[12] who had had a dramatic conversion from Shamanism (a form of white magic) to Christianity. The 'bad' was represented by a very sad woman, deep into black magic, who openly talked about her out-of-body sexual exploits, and clearly believed that she was living under a curse which would kill her in a few years' time. The pagans danced cheerfully around spring fires, prayed in circles with strange incantations in tongues unknown to me and portrayed themselves as pleasantly harmless.

In this chaos, the forces of darkness must allow themselves an evil cackle. Disbelieving in the devil may be theologically fashionable, but it is pastorally absurd.

Theologically, if there is no spiritual opposition, no fallen angels, then God stands accused of having made an appalling world. Recently, I watched a TV programme on the Congo, in which there was a long section on the behaviour of gorillas. For the most part, they seemed much more pleasant, and far more caring, than many human beings.

My reaction was somewhat confirmed by watching, a few days later, a horrific documentary on the extermination of the Jews in the Second World War, and the part played by the outwardly charming Adolf Eichmann. If there is no spiritual opposition, then the mess that humankind is in has to be explained almost entirely because of human greed, selfishness and sexual desires.

As we shall see in the next chapter, there is a lot of evidence that Satan exists. There is evidence that evil spirits, and other spiritual forces, can sometimes inhabit people and buildings. If people come to us with psychic problems, they need compassionate help. If the church fails to take them seriously, it cannot be surprised if people go to spiritualists or to anyone else who will listen to their problems.

At the moment, the church seems reluctant to engage publicly with these issues. Diocesan exorcists exist but their vital work is usually hidden away. Obviously, no one is advocating a blaze of self-seeking publicity, but Jesus has given us the answer to these dark matters and we should be sharing this good news with a troubled society. When the Gerasene demoniac (Mark 5:1–20) was set free from a legion of evil spirits, Jesus sent him back to his own village with the words: 'Tell them how much the Lord has done for you'.

Jesus' ministry initiated a clear conflict between light and darkness, the kingdom of God, and the kingdom of Satan. Likewise, the epistles have a number of classic passages about spiritual warfare, and the final book of the Bible, the Revelation of John, paints a vivid picture of heavenly battles – past, present and future. Jesus was explicit about the reality of Satan. He was also quite clear that

Satan has an army of angels – many of whom appear as evil spirits.

For the Christian, this settles the question. For anyone seriously searching for the truth, the Christian explanation dispels the confusion caused by a dubious and dangerous intertwining of angelic and psychic experiences.

Notes

1. Dr H.C. Moolenburgh, *Meetings with Angels*, C.W. Daniel, 1992, p. 143.
2. Richard Webster, *Spirit Guides and Angel Guardians*, Llewellyn Publications, 2001.
3. Hope Price, *Angels*, London: Macmillan, 1993, p. 5.
4. Laeh Maggie Garfield and Jack Grant, *Angels and Companions in Spirit*, Celestial Arts, 1984, pp. 90–99.
5. Other warning texts and stories include: Leviticus 19:31; Isaiah 47:8–15; Malachi 3:5; Acts 13:8; Revelation 22:15, not to mention Jesus' encounter with Satan (who also specializes in quoting Scripture for his own benefit – see Matthew 4:1–11). These should convince anyone prepared to take the Bible seriously that any book, which approves of and encourages psychic phenomena, is teaching something dangerous.
6. *Sylvia Browne's Book of Angels*, Hay House, 2003.
7. Doreen Virtue, *Healing with the Angels*, Hay House, 2005.
8. Philip Pullmann's famous trilogy *His Dark Materials*, London: Point, 1995, is a powerful example of this genre which is unusually powerfully anti-Christian in its underlying philosophy.
9. Moolenburgh, *Ibid*. p. 1.
10. Cindy Jacobs, *Possessing the Gates of the Enemy*, Grand Rapids: Zondervan, 1994, pp. 138–143.
11. See John Woolmer, *Angels*, Oxford: Monarch, 2003, pp. 230–232.
12. See John Woolmer, *Angels*, Oxford: Monarch, 2003, Chapter 10 for Deborah Wearing's powerful testimony.

CHAPTER 9

Angels in Opposition

THE BIBLE IS STRANGELY SILENT about the origin of Satan. After the serpent slithers off the stage, Satan seldom appears in the Old Testament. By contrast, Jesus' ministry initiates a clear conflict between light and darkness, the kingdom of God, and the kingdom of Satan. Jesus taught that Satan was a fallen angel; he taught that Satan had angels under his command; he acknowledged the existence of evil spirits which could partially control individuals; frequently, he took authority over them and expelled them. Here is one account, right at the beginning of what is probably the oldest written Gospel recorded from the preaching of Peter in Rome by Mark in about AD 64:

They went to Capernaum, and when the Sabbath came, Jesus went into the synagogue and began to teach. The people were amazed at his teaching, because he taught them as one who had authority, not as the teachers of the law. Just then a man in their synagogue who was possessed by an evil spirit cried out, 'What do you want with us, Jesus of Nazareth? Have you come to destroy us? I know who you are – the Holy One of God!'

'Be quiet!' said Jesus sternly. 'Come out of him!' The evil spirit shook the man violently and came out of him with a shriek.

The people were all so amazed that they asked each other, 'What is this? A new teaching – and with authority! He even gives orders to evil spirits and they obey him.' News about him spread quickly over the whole region of Galilee. (Mark 1:21–28)

The conflict, which had begun in the wilderness (see Mark 1:12–13), had exploded in Jesus' first recorded day of ministry. The conflict continues throughout his ministry of healing and deliverance – for instance Jesus heals a crippled woman 'whom Satan has kept bound for eighteen long years' (Luke 13:16). The mission of the seventy-two (see Luke 10:1–24) is particularly revealing about Jesus' strategy and understanding of Satan. He gives his workers authority to proclaim that 'the kingdom of God is near you' (10:9). When they return in triumph, they declare, 'Lord, even the demons submit to us in your name' (10:17). Jesus replied, 'I saw Satan fall like lightning from heaven. I have given you authority to trample on snakes and scorpions and to overcome all the power of the enemy; nothing will harm you' (10:18–19).

Jesus knew that Satan had fallen from heaven; Jesus knew that the he had authority over the demons; Jesus knew that he could delegate that authority to others who acted in his name. In the parable of the sheep and the goats, Jesus refers to 'the devil *and his angels*' (Matthew 25:41, my italics). In the Gospels, the devil's angels show up as evil spirits.

Evil spirits today?

In the twenty-first century, evil spirits get a bad press. A number of criminal trials in the UK have resulted from people using terrible cruelty to try and beat evil spirits out

of unfortunate children. It is not surprising that responsible
people rush to condemn any form of 'deliverance' ministry.
In the last forty years, there have been a small number of well
publicized cases where such ministry has gone badly wrong;
there have also been situations where serious pastoral mis-
judgments have been made and people who have personality
problems have been encouraged to undergo deliverance
ministry by misguided enthusiasts. Nevertheless, there are
many situations where people do need this ministry and
where they are very grateful when they have been set free.
Here are two examples from my own experience.

The man who came to dinner
Some years ago, my wife and I were entertaining a psychiatrist and her husband to dinner. The psychiatrist was a
Christian, her husband an interested agnostic. We were
talking about the reality of evil when the doorbell rang. The
clergy, when at home, are never off-duty. I sighed and went
to the door. A large, tall ex-marine, a man I will call James,
came into the house and collapsed unable to talk. He told
me to get on with my dinner party.

After about twenty minutes, he came and joined us and
said the problem was that he had just beaten up his wife. He
asked me to go and see if she was all right. I knew the family slightly, as I had recently baptized their three children.
Rather reluctantly, I left the table and cycled round to his
house. His wife greeted me. She was quite calm and
remarked that James was 'a binge drinker and that these
things happen'. She told me to go back to my guests! I can't
have been away more than half an hour. When I returned to
my house, there was an interesting scene.

The dining room table was on its side, James was

growling and gnawing at one of the legs, four policemen were trying to restrain him, a neighbour was looking uncomfortable, the psychiatrist and her husband had retreated into the relative safety of a nearby alcove and my wife was looking remarkably calm.

Eventually, James calmed down and the police proposed taking him to the cells for the night – so that he couldn't do any more damage! When he was calm, I asked him if he had ever been involved any occult activity. His temporary calm disappeared, and he snarled at me that he'd 'used Ouija when in the merchant navy'. He calmed down again and the police carted him off for a night in the cells.

I was able to see him over the next few days. He agreed to let his doctor treat him for binge drinking. I told his doctor, who was also mine, that there was an underlying spiritual problem which would also need sorting out. James started to come to church.

About six months later, he was sitting in my garden talking to me. He said, 'I don't really feel comfortable in church – it's as though there is a sort of cloud over me.' I told him that, in order to feel at peace, he needed to make a clear renunciation of the past and a commitment to Jesus.

We went inside to my study. He was sitting on a very solid chair (which I am sitting on today as I write). After a short time, his face changed and he gasped out, 'You had better pray quickly!' Before I could do anything, he started to shake violently, the chair split and he landed on the floor amidst a characteristically untidy heap of papers. I remembered that Michael Green, my rector, was away writing, *'I believe in Satan's downfall'* and my other two colleagues were playing cricket for the diocese.

Feeling very alone, I prayed – commanding the prostrate

six-foot plus ex-marine to stop shaking in the name of the Lord. To my immense relief, James calmed down. We spent the next hour threading our way through the Oxford rush-hour traffic to remove an Ouija board from the potting shed on his allotment.

A few days later, with the permission of the bishop and the knowledge of his doctor, a few of us met in the local church to pray for James. I led him through the service of renewal of vows of baptism. I took the vows in the reverse order – beginning with *'Do you renounce evil?'* For a while, James couldn't speak, then he started to shake, gripping the pew so hard that I though it might break. After a short time, he shouted that he renounced evil and made a full confession of all occult things that he had been involved with, and continued with repentance and a public commitment to Jesus. He described it as like a light coming on in his life.

For some years things went well. He became very involved and valued by the church; his family started to come to church. Very sadly, some years later (long after I had moved from the area), he left his wife and family. I don't think that this was anything to do with the previous problems, but it is reminder to us all of how fragile faith and commitment can be even after powerful experiences of God's love and human forgiveness.

The strangler fig

Occasionally, people are trapped by powerful experiences, without even realizing what has happened to them. A few years ago, I had the privilege of praying with a woman, whom it is best not to name (I write with her permission), a refugee from an African country. Her heartbreaking story, in summary, was this:

My parents had difficulty in conceiving. After fifteen years, they went to a witch doctor. His spells were efficacious and I was born. Aged fourteen, I was sent to my future mother-in-law's house. She, knowing my parents' difficulties, took me to a witch doctor so that I would conceive. My husband was a successful businessman. I was so ill after the birth of my first child that I ran home to my parents. They sent me back.

My husband went into politics. He was on the side of the government, and had quite a prominent position. He accompanied me to the hospital when I was pregnant with my second child. He was disgusted by the state of the hospital, and tried to get something done politically. When my third child was born, he found there had been no improvement. He joined the opposition.

On New Year's Day 1997, we were arrested. He was effectively told to keep out of politics or be killed. He was very determined and wouldn't be silenced. In May 1997, he was murdered in police custody. I, and my youngest two children, were helped to escape to England. My eldest is still in hiding in the African country.

For five years, she has struggled to make a new life in England. She has been helped by good Christian friends. She made much progress, but was locked into grief, self-pity and anger. One afternoon, I met her with a discerning friend who has provided some testimony about angels (see page 34).

When we began to pray, the main problem appeared to be her inability to forgive. She needed to forgive the President, the police, her husband ('if he hadn't been so obstinate this needn't have happened'), her mother-in-law and her parents. We made little progress until, by the Holy Spirit, a word which was the name of the witch doctor's controlling spirit (the one her parents went to) was revealed. I wrote the word, an African sounding word of about seven letters, on a piece of paper. She changed the sixth letter from 't' to 'b'.

As soon as that happened, she was transformed. 'That's it!' she screamed, and behaved for a few minutes like a powerful witch doctor – screaming, chanting and displaying blazing eyes. After some quiet prayer, the spirit was released. She slept for the next week, and soon afterwards was able to pray to forgive all those who had hurt her. We made the important distinction between forgiveness and justice – we could pray for justice, but still pray for forgiveness for those who had murdered her husband.

This story illustrates my point that occult problems cling very deeply to people, and make it hard for them to receive Christ in the first place, and to forgive others. My friend had received Christ, but couldn't make any real spiritual progress because of her grief and understandable anger.

Two years later, her eldest son was brought out of her country – remarkably by one of her husband's political opponents! She celebrated this great event with a splendid party attended by many members of her church community.

Her experience reminds me of the strangler figs in Africa. A large bird, often a hornbill, drops the seed of a fig in the crown of a growing tree. The fig takes root and slowly grows downwards. It is not particularly dangerous, just unsightly, until years later it reaches the ground and takes root. At this stage, the host tree is in real danger of destruction.

Indwelling Spirits are rare

I want to stress that it is very rare for human beings to be invaded by evil spirits[1]. I have seen a number of people in different parts of the world set free by prayer in the name of Jesus. Usually the process is simple, gentle and clear; occasionally it is complicated, quite violent and powerful. The causes of the problem are almost always somewhat of occult involvement, occasionally the involvement comes from ancestors or partners. The normal process of prayer involves specific renunciation of whatever involvement the person has had with dark things, repentance and turning to Christ.

Here are a few more examples – given, in headline, for reasons of brevity and anonymity.

I was called to a house, where several clergy were trying to help a woman who was sitting in the cloakroom hissing. After a long while, she emerged and tried to tell me her story. The most obvious and deepest stress was that she was being stalked by someone whom she trusted but had no desire for a relationship with. The second problem was that she had recently been prayed for to receive the gift of speaking in tongues. She had started speaking in a new language, but nobody liked the sound of it or felt that it was a gift from God!

It also emerged that as a teenager, some twenty years earlier, she had been involved with fairly minor occult practices. As she calmed down, we took her through prayers of renunciation of anything occult and anything that she had experienced that was not of God, through prayers of repentance and forgiveness towards the man who was troubling her, and finally a re-commitment of her faith in Christ. Although there were periods of hesitation, and occasionally her eyes went wild and she looked fearful, all this was accomplished fairly easily. We anointed her, on the forehead, with oil as a sign of the presence of the Holy Spirit, and she felt very different. It seems as if the occult stuff opened a crack for the powers of evil to get into her which widened considerably under the emotional pressure. I believe that she is now doing very well.

Once when preaching in a very rural part of Zambia, a member of the Mother's Union, who was beautifully dressed in her blue and white uniform, fell out of the pew screaming. I had been preaching about the powerful ministry of Philip, in Acts 8, just before the angel of the Lord sent him off to meet the Ethiopian in the desert. I decided to stop my sermon (I had said quite enough!) and accompanied her as she was carried out of the church kicking and screaming.

We placed her on the ground in the shade and waited for her to calm down. The temptation is to start shouting at the demons, but this only makes matters worse! When she was calmer, I asked her to name the spirits who were troubling her. She mentioned a few familiar Zambian spirit names. I then asked her to renounce them, tell them in the name of Jesus to depart and to breathe in the power and presence of the Holy Spirit. Very soon, she was smiling!

A few hours later, like Peter's mother-in-law (see Mark 1:31) she helped to serve us lunch. It was then that I realized that she was the wife of the local priest. He had carried on with the service, completely calmly, while we had been praying with his wife!

There are several common threads which run through all these stories. Previous occult involvement either by the person or within their family past or present is normal. Most people with these problems have wild and troubled eyes, they often display unusual strength and frequently speak in strange languages. Obviously there are plenty of cases of people with psychiatric disorders who display these types of symptoms and we need to be *very cautious* before leaping in with spiritual diagnoses.

Sometimes people's spiritual problems were caused by their partners or their ancestors. I have met several people with husbands or ancestors who were deep into Freemasonry who displayed all the normal signs of some sort of demonization. I am not suggesting for one moment that all Freemasons have this problem; but within the higher arches of Freemasonry oaths are taken to the strange 'God' called Jahbulon and even at an elementary level blood-curdling threats are made to those who betray Masonic secrets.

One woman told me that her daughter often dreamt of being strangled which is similar to one part of a ritual of initiation which involves being blindfolded and having a noose around one's neck. The woman herself, a strong Christian, displayed extraordinary demonic manifestations when talking about her husband's involvement. Of course, many Masons are Christian worshippers and are totally unaware of, or blind to, the potential spiritual problems caused by their dual allegiance.

Problems with buildings

A surprisingly large number of people seem to encounter problems with strange presences in buildings. There seem to be several main reasons for this type of phenomena. First, there will be natural explanations for some strange happenings. Secondly, there are places where unpleasant things have happened in the past and there has been no prayer or spiritual ministry to quiet the unhappy memories. Thirdly, there are people who because of their own psychic presence cause strange things to happen more or less wherever they go. Fourthly, there are places where weird things happen for which no rational or spiritual explanation can be found (that doesn't meant to say there isn't an explanation!).

One diocesan exorcist testifying publicly, in a TV programme, stated that every situation that he had been asked to investigate turned out to have a natural, rational explanation. He cited creaking floorboards caused by faulty heating systems and the like. Personally, almost every situation that I have been asked about appears to have had a genuine psychic problem, although I haven't always discovered a reason for the trouble. Here are some typical examples.

A tale of two pubs

Two pubs about five miles apart were both experiencing strange things. One of them claimed to have the corpse of a notorious highwayman buried under the bar. The only evidence for this was that the man was known to have been executed very close to the site of the pub. Some years ago, the landlord called me in because his young children were having nightmares. We prayed through the pub, especially in the area where the burial was supposed to be. One of my team felt freezing cold in one place (this is quite a common experience); apart from that the visit was uneventful.

However, two very positive things happened. The children started to sleep properly and two of our healing team went in to pray for the landlord's son. He was suffering from severe eczema and they had tried many different treatments. After prayer, he was dramatically healed.

The second pub had a reputation for being haunted. I did discover that a recent vicar had been alcoholic (reputed to baptize babies in the name of the Father, the Son and the Bristol Water Board) and that one of his children and others were reputed to have had Ouija board sessions in an upper room in the pub. A succession of landlords had a disastrous tenancy. Alcoholism, depression, suicide followed one another in a quick sequence.

A number of people told me of strange things that they had experienced. These included a senior church lawyer who, as a sceptical teenager, recorded the sounds of an alleged ghost! A new landlord came, and I offered to exorcize or bless the pub.

He laughed and said it was a load of nonsense. I said that his was the second best solution. What I meant was that the problem needed dealing with, but if he didn't believe in such things he probably wouldn't be troubled. So it proved to be. The church made a conscious to effort to use the pub for occasional harvest events and regular suppers; the landlord, who did die younger than average, had a successful tenancy for nearly twenty years, and the spiritual atmosphere seemed to become quiet.

Troubled stables

This account was written for me by the late Anne Goode. She became a great friend, partly as a result of what she recounts:

I had just moved to Somerset. We had bought an overpriced attractive eighteenth-century building which was immediately opposite the site of an annual pop festival which was growing in international importance. I was aware of an atmosphere of menace which was affecting my family. My academically brilliant husband began behaving oddly, displaying signs of early dementia; my musically gifted son was being bullied at school; my daughter spent all her time like a ghost child, pale and withdrawn, in the stables and I was prone to uncontrollable outbursts of rage which upset the whole family.

In spiritual and emotional disarray, I sought the help of John Woolmer whose recently published book, *Growing up to Salvation*, contained a chapter about the occult which I read with surprise and relief. During prayer, which included the laying-on of hands, I experienced liquid light flowing through my whole body. I found that I was totally free of the dark fear which had gripped every area of my life. Problems within the house still needed dealing with, but I was no longer afraid and family life improved. The church began to use the house for staff days, but I sensed that the house needed deeper ministry than the simple blessing that had been given to it.

After the mysterious death in the field of one of my daughter's horses, John decided, during a staff day, to perform a full-scale exorcism of the whole premises, complete with a large jug of holy water (water that had been set aside by prayer for this purpose). My daughter and I were particularly troubled by unpleasant graffiti on the stable walls which seemed to imply somewhat sinister use by previous occupants. I felt that the evil presence had been around the buildings for a long time.

The staff team eventually gathered around the stable which had been previously occupied by the dead horse, and they stood in a semi-circle. John entered the stables, prayed in tongues, and tipped half a jug of water on the straw, commanding any evil presence to leave in the name of Jesus. One of the staff members, not used to this sort of thing, visibly jumped backwards and described how a huge force leaving the stables seemed to hit him at the moment of the prayer.

The results of the prayer were beneficial. Visitors, and there are many of them, invariably comment on the peace and beauty of the place.

All that happened about twenty years ago, Anne remained a good friend until her peaceful and quite remarkable death in 2004. She suffered from an unpleasant form of cancer, but was wonderfully looked after by her family and church, and died in her sleep on Christmas night, twenty-four hours after attending the midnight communion in the church I used to lead.

Troubled houses

Many people seem to suffer spiritual disturbance in their homes. Space prevents me giving any detailed examples. But, in headline, one family, total unbelievers in this sort of thing, heard footsteps on non-existent stairs, and doors opening and closing. As a result they were quite frightened. It turned out that over a hundred years earlier, a mother who lived in the house died quite young. Her son, who lived with her, was so distraught that he attempted to extricate her from her grave in the nearby churchyard. He was carted off to an asylum. Prayers said for him and his mother to be at peace quickly restored sanity to the household.

In another disturbed house, there had been an early and unexpected death and various other strange happenings.

Three nearby houses had also suffered premature deaths – all of men in their fifties. We found a well in the garden, which was very close to the other properties, in which a body had been discovered. The deceased person in the well was probably a victim of murder. Suicide didn't seem likely and an accident almost impossible. As we prayed, the local vicar heard a hissing sound, and it seems that peace was restored.

In a town house, a pregnant woman was aware of a sinister presence at the top of the stairs. She had only just moved in; her husband felt no such problems. We did some investigations and found that about ten years earlier the owner had been murdered at the top of the stairs by a schizophrenic lodger.

A friend of mine, with no prior knowledge of the situation, prayed around the house for a few minutes. She reported sensing three things – first that the house was very unfriendly to women; secondly that something had happened on the landing; thirdly that there was a small room beside the landing which had problems. The first two statements were obviously true and we concluded that the third room had probably been used, by either the owner or the lodger, for some strange spiritual activities. After prayer, the whole situation calmed down.

Sometime later, I met another family who had lived in the house earlier. They reported that they had had no strange encounters, but that one of their young children had complained of seeing someone on the stairs.

Once in one of my former parishes, a distraught man called because he and his partner had seen apparitions and claimed to have taken a video of things moving around his bedroom. He never managed to show me the video, and it became clear that his problem was mainly due to alcohol. If there were psychic disturbances, it was his personality that was the cause. It would have been easy to waste a lot of time listening to someone who had no real desire to change!

By contrast, another family called me to a farmhouse where they were aware of tobacco and experiencing some other strange happenings. No one in the family smoked. It turned out that the previous owner, who was a strong smoker, had committed suicide. After prayers, and a household communion service, everything became quiet. The family were particularly grateful as they needed to move and prior to the service no one would even consider buying the house. They made a satisfactory sale soon afterwards.

Place memories

Sometimes memories from the very distant past seem to affect buildings. Once, I prayed in a room where a teenage girl claimed that she had seen, on several occasions, a fully clad Roman soldier on her bed – this would seem highly fanciful except for the coincidental fact that she lived in a house built very close to an ancient Roman road called the Fosse Way. About ten years earlier, there had been a redevelopment of the land. Skeletons of a large number of Roman citizens of the fourth century were uncovered, taken for forensic analysis, and eventually reburied in the local churchyard.

On another occasion in Papua New Guinea, I was called to the house of a missionary. They were living in a modern house, built into the side of a hill. The whole area was now part of a large Christian mission station. Up to about forty

years ago, it had been disputed ground between two war-
ring tribes. Their teenage children had bedrooms on the
lowest floor which would have been below ground level in
the past.

Recently their very intelligent teenage daughter had
admitted to being frightened by strange presences in her
bedroom which had occurred over a period of about eight
years. Their younger teenage son also said that from time to
time he, too, had been troubled. A number of us prayed
throughout the house and sensed God's presence and peace.
Shortly afterwards, the daughter who had been struggling
with her faith for a number of years, made her first clear
profession of commitment to Jesus.

While I cannot be certain, I am inclined to think that the
house was built on a place where there had been fierce
fighting – probably involving death and cannibalism. The
daughter, who knew people who had been involved with
Ouija boards (yes, such things can happen even on Mission
stations!) had never done anything like that herself and I am
sure that the presence in her bedroom was in no way
brought about by anything that she had done.

Over the years, I have visited many houses where the
occupants were troubled by strange phenomena. They
always seemed relieved to discover that *they were not alone
in having this sort of trouble*. Usually there was some sort of
reason of the type that I have indicated in the preceding stories. Invariably, peace to the building and to the residents
came after a few visits. Occasionally, I could find no sort of
spiritual explanation, but prayer still brought peace and
harmony. Here is an example.

A *distraught factory manager*

A small factory set on an industrial estate in a city had recently changed hands. The new manager was making medical equipment with a small but dedicated staff. They were being distracted and frightened by a number of phenomena. These included strange smells, people hearing footsteps especially on a staircase, inexplicable electrical failures, a large girder, which had seemed securely attached, crashing to the ground, a door set on a code being opened at night and when the manager who was alone in the factory went to investigate, he found no sign of anyone. There was also a sense of evil and darkness in parts of the factory. Workmen who had come in to do electrical work had been terrified. One employee was particularly sensitive and bothered by a whole series of disturbing events.

The previous owner had mentioned that he was having trouble in his new workplace and there was another factory within a quarter of a mile where I discovered that similar things had happened a few years earlier. We couldn't find any explanation. The factory was built where there had previously been fields, and although I felt the previous owner might have contributed to the atmosphere this seemed an insufficient explanation. The troubles seemed to be a mixture of childish misbehaviour and something more sinister. It took three sessions of prayer, culminating with a communion service on the factory floor, to bring calm and peace. A year later, all was reported to be peaceful and the business to be doing well.

What are we to make of all of this?

Three main explanations are usually offered for these strange situations in buildings – place memories, unquiet dead and misuse of the building (or territory) for occult purposes. The Old Testament gives many examples of 'high places' where false cults practised and led the Israelites astray and which had to be cleansed by action by prophets or kings. Hezekiah (2 Kings 18:1–4) removed high places, smashed sacred stones, cut down poles used in cultic worship and even destroyed the famous bronze serpent which Moses had made (see Numbers 21:9 and John 3:14). The famous serpent had become an idol and an object of false worship.

There are no examples of place memories remotely similar to the story above of the Roman soldier in the bedroom. Nor are there any convincing stories of the unquiet dead. The strange account of Saul visiting the Witch of Endor (see 1 Samuel 28) has puzzled theologians as wise as Augustine. No one seems sure if the spirit that the witch called up was really the prophet Samuel or an evil entity pretending to be him. One thing is certain, the outcome was disastrous for King Saul and he would have been far wiser not to enquire of a witch!

I am agnostic about some of the causes of problems in buildings, but I am certain that the problems are real. I am also certain that prayer, said in the name, and with the authority, of Jesus Christ, through the power of his cross and resurrection is highly effective. Paul puts it with his customary clarity:

... having disarmed the powers and authorities, he made a public spectacle of them, triumphing over them by the cross. (Colossians 2:15)

What have angels to do with these matters?

Four things need to be said. First, in most situations, we are dealing with a real spiritual problem. People need help and, in some way, many of them have touched, heard, sensed or seen something which has no rational explanation. Usually, they have been very frightened, or they have frightened other people.

Secondly, we need to remember that Satan can only *imitate and not create*. Psychic spiritual 'gifts' are a distortion of the spiritual gifts recorded in 1 Corinthians 12. For instance, clairvoyance and foretelling the future are distortions of the gifts of knowledge and prophecy. If God reveals to me the name of a controlling Spirit (see p. 186) that is quite different from some psychic experience involving visualizing angels or other sorts of forbidden knowledge. True spiritual gifts are only given to set people free, psychic gifts tend to trap people into self-fulfilling prophecy and into fear. God made everything – and gave both the spiritual world and humankind freewill. Any evil entities are a fallen part of *his* created order.

Thirdly, the name of Jesus has extraordinary authority and power when used correctly. In the New Testament, in Acts 19 there is a detailed account of Paul's mission in Ephesus. At one stage, some Jewish exorcists realized that there was power in the name of Jesus. Seven of them tried to cast out an evil spirit in the name of Jesus. The result was dramatic:

> ... the evil spirit answered them, 'Jesus I know, and I
> know about Paul, but who are you?' Then the man who
> had the evil spirit jumped on them and overpowered
> them all. He gave them such a beating that they ran out
> of the house naked and bleeding. (Acts 19:15–16)

The main consequence of this entertaining drama was that
the name of Jesus was held in high repute; many people
became Christians, and there was a huge bonfire when
many occult scrolls were burnt!

As we have seen the name of Jesus also cleanses buildings – the account above of the cleansing of Anne's stables
has no possible psychological explanation. Either my colleague is a liar (and I can vouch for him as one of the most
upright and truthful men that I know) or the huge force,
which he felt and visibly reacted to, was expelled from the
stables as a result of prayer in the name of Jesus.

Fourthly, since Jesus alone has this authority, we would
be *very foolish to reject his explanation*. He refers to 'the devil
and his angels' (Matthew 25:41). He also refers to Satan as
the prince of this world (see John 12:31, 14:30, 16:11). Evil
spirits are a reality and part of the angelic fall. What a terrible transformation from a beautiful bringer of messages
from God to a miserable messenger of the devil!

Some fallen angels have reappeared as demons; others are
involved in what Paul calls the battle 'against the spiritual
forces of evil in the heavenly realms' (Ephesians 6:12). Some
fallen angels are also called 'deceiving spirits' (1 Timothy 4:1).
As such, they seek to cause more chaos than their rather
more obvious counterparts which I have been writing about.

This explanation of the existence and origin of evil spirits
is both biblical and experiential. Any other explanation drives

us either into Dualism (two equal and opposite powers) or into denial of the existence of the power and reality of evil.

Every time we see a small victory against the dark powers, we are reminded of the far greater victory won on the first Easter Day, and the final victory to be won when 'the Son of Man is going to come in his Father's glory with his angels' (see Matthew 16:27). That is the great Christian hope. This hope, which is well supported, by the evidence from this chapter, and many similar testimonies, is based on the power of the name of Jesus.

> ... at the name of Jesus every knee should bow, in heaven and on earth and under the earth, and every tongue confess that Jesus Christ is Lord, to the glory of God the Father. (Philippians 2:10–11)

This victory was made certain at Calvary, on the first Good Friday; but will remain incomplete until the end of time as we know it. A German pastor, Oscar Cullmann, was ministering in Germany in 1944. He realized that when the allies landed in Normandy the war was effectively over, but that much fighting still had to take place. He saw this as an analogy of the spiritual situation which we are all now caught up in.

It is, of course, much more comfortable to believe that all angels are doing good; but the powerful witness of Jesus, and 2,000 years of the Christian era, prove otherwise.

Note

1. See John Woolmer, *Healing and Deliverance*, Oxford: Monarch, 1999 for an in-depth discussion of this important and controversial topic (see especially pp. 32–35, 264–266 and throughout).

CHAPTER 10

Angel Questions

1. How do we know if an angel is from God?

Paul, writing to the Galatians, says: 'But even if we or an angel from heaven should preach a gospel other than the one we preached to you, let him be eternally condemned!' (Galatians 1:8). We noted (p. 170) how easily false stories about the second coming of Jesus emerge from spurious angelic encounters. The test of the truth of any spiritual encounter (angelic, visionary, dream, guidance) is found by considering these three questions.

Does the encounter honour Jesus? Does it agree with his teaching? What fruit has it brought into people's lives? If the answer to the first two questions is yes and there is good fruit, then the angel is almost certainly from God. If the 'angel' gives teaching that is contrary to the Bible or about unknown areas (such as the timing of Jesus' return) it is almost certainly not from God. Remember that the devil is the father of lies (John 8:44) and will do his utmost to deceive us.

2. Why does God allow fallen angels to operate?

Presumably it is part of his gift of freedom of choice to all creation. We are not told how the angels fell (there are hints in the Old Testament – see Isaiah 14:12–15 and Ezekiel 28:11–19). The strong implication of these texts is that pride was the root cause. But we are told by Jesus (and others) that the angelic rebellion did happen.

No theology of suffering, of natural disasters, or of sin makes any sense without some understanding that there is spiritual opposition. If there is no Satan, and no fallen angels, then belief in God becomes very difficult and the cross becomes an unnecessary tragedy. The age-old problem of suffering makes belief very hard at the best of times; but it becomes intolerable if there is no spiritual opposition.

Ultimately, despite fallen angels, God remains in total control, but traditional Christian theology provides a way through the gloom of human sin and suffering. The cross becomes the place of victory over evil, the supreme example of overcoming suffering, and the means of releasing humankind from the guilt of sin.

3. Why do some people think that a third of the angels are fallen? Are fallen angels organized?

Revelation 12:4 says that the dragon (Satan) swept a third of the stars out of heaven. Some people make this calculation based on this verse. Jesus referred to 'The devil and his angels' as does the book of Revelation. Thus we may safely conclude that Satan has an army of angels, who we experience mainly as evil spirits. To assume that they number a third of the whole is somewhat speculative.

We do not how this rebellious army is organized. Some Christians believe in what they call 'Territorial Spirits'. There is some biblical evidence for this. Anecdotally, my encounter in Zambia (see the opening chapter) felt like a battle with territorial powers.

In the Acts of the Apostles, there are powerful spiritual conflicts with a sorcerer in Samaria (Acts 8:4–25), with another sorcerer in Cyprus (Acts 13:6–12), with a fortune-teller controlled by her owners for their financial gain (Acts

16:16–19) and with the cult of the goddess Diana in Ephesus (Acts 19:11–41). In other places, the opposition powers were more subtle. In Athens (Acts 17:16–34), there was no spiritual battle. Mockery proved a more powerful weapon, and there were few converts and no church was established.

What is clear is that there is a powerful spiritual opposition which will *ultimately be defeated at the end of time as we know it.*

4. Who has a guardian angel?

Jesus implied that children have angels in heaven (Matthew 18:10). This verse and Psalms 91:11 and 34:7 support a belief in guardian angels. The early church clearly believed (whether correctly or not is less clear) that Peter had a guardian angel (the biblical account in Acts 12 suggests the angel was sent directly by God rather than a guardian angel on long-term sentry duty). In the pages of the Bible and throughout history, good people have been killed in battle, suffered accidents and been killed by persecution.

Christians rely on the indwelling presence of the Holy Spirit as their normal means of guidance, protection, communication with and from God. Angelic experiences are the exception not the norm; but this doesn't mean that angels are not constantly around us. Elisha (2 Kings 6:16) was able to see 'beyond the veil'. After prayer, his servant's eyes were also opened and in tune with the spiritual world.

5. Is it right to pray for angelic protection?

Many people do in times of real danger; Psalm 34:7 encourages me to believe for angelic protection for my household. Psalm 91:11 (which was quoted out of context by the devil when Jesus was being tempted) promises protection to those who put their trust in God. Praying for God's protection would, for many people, quite naturally include asking for angelic cover.

What is clear from the Bible is that angels operate entirely under God's command. Psalm 103:20 says, 'Praise the LORD, you his angels, you mighty ones who do his bidding, who obey his word.' We should pray for God's protection; we may I think request angelic assistance. Most of the time this will be *unseen*; but the evidence when angels have revealed themselves is sufficiently encouraging for us to have confidence in their presence – seen or unseen.

6. Why does God sometimes send angels and sometimes send the Holy Spirit?

The Acts of the Apostles has a number of examples of direct communication between God and the leading members of the church – he uses various means including dreams and visions, angels and the Holy Spirit. Sometimes he uses natural means (such as the persecution which followed the martyrdom of Stephen) to get the church to change course. In the Acts, angels appear at very special times such as the Ascension, the imprisonment of the apostles, getting Philip to leave a succesful mission and to go on a special journey, enabling Peter and Cornelius (the first Gentile convert) to connect, rescuing Peter and strengthening Paul in times of acute danger.

Angels tend to occur in a cluster of stories in the Bible – for instance in the latter part of Abraham's life, in the Elijah–Elisha cycle and in Daniel. They also occur at the beginning and end of Jesus' life but relatively little during his normal life and ministry.

In the pages of the Bible, angels never seem to appear to

deal with *the small or the mundane* – which is in sharp contrast to much modern literature on the subject. I cannot stress too strongly that the Holy Spirit, who dwells in all believers, is *God's normal means of communication*.

7. If people are not protected by angels is something wrong with them spiritually?

Emphatically not! Jesus said (Luke 13:1–4) that those on whom the tower in Siloam fell were no more wicked (or blessed) than anyone else. We live in a fallen world, a world in which creation groans (Romans 8:18ff.) and we are all vulnerable to natural disasters, accidents, disease, warfare… Christians are liable to be involved in accidents.

Some years ago, George Hoffmann who was doing a wonderful work as the National Director of Tear Fund was killed walking across a road to visit someone.

In 2005, there was an air crash in Papua New Guinea. The two pilots, Chris and Richard who worked for the Missionary Aviation Fellowship were killed. They were much loved; people travelled vast distances to come to their memorial service. A friend told me this story:

Three men walked five days through the jungle to come to Chris and Richard's memorial service. They had no food on the third night and after walking through the fourth day and having not come across any villages on their journey, had little strength left for the last day's journey. The three built a small fire and one of the men prayed: 'Lord hear us. You provided for Elijah, so you can also provide for us. We need food.' Fifteen minutes later a man walked out of the jungle and handed the man who had prayed a huge taro (taro is the favourite vegetable of many of the New Guinea tribes). He turned around and walked back into the jungle without speaking one word.   The taro was so large, that when the men had cooked it there was plenty left over, they couldn't finish it... and believe me... Papua New Guinean men can out eat anyone I have ever seen, and I have seen some of the youth eat!!!   Was it a man, or an angel?

I cannot begin to speculate why the three local men should receive assistance while the pilots died. The evidence for God's sovereign hand is overwhelming and we have to accept his will. The end of the book of Job includes the challenge from God:

> Will the one who contends with the Almighty correct him? Let him who accuses God answer him! (Job 40:2)

8. Is it wrong to try and visualize angels?
It depends what you mean. Some people think that they are aware of the presence of angels: hearing them singing, sensing their presence in worship. They may well imagine what the angels look like – this is quite different from trying to conjure up the sight of an angel by using our spiritual imagination.

9. What are spirit guides?
Spirit guides occur in lots of modern books about angels. They are generally seen as belonging to a lower order than angels. People are encouraged to find them, work with them and listen to them. *They do not occur in the Bible.*

I have read a number of books which have included 'guidance' from spirit guides. Much of the actual guidance, even from a practical angle, seems highly dubious (see chapter 8).

From a Christian perspective, the answer is simple – spirit guides are a form of deception and should be avoided at all costs. They pretend to be messengers from God, subtly replacing the work of the Holy Spirit.

10. Are there hierarchies of angels?

The Bible recognizes different types of spiritual being. One archangel, Michael, is named (see Revelation 12:7, Jude 9 and Daniel 10:13,21 and 12:1). Gabriel is named on a number of occasions. Gabriel is described as an angel (Luke 1:11–20 and 1:26–38) and as the man 'I had seen in the earlier vision' in Daniel 8:16–26 and 9:20–27. The Angel of the Lord, who sometimes seems almost interchangeable with God himself, turns up quite frequently. Cherubim and seraphim are mentioned occasionally. Paul mentions thrones without explaining what they are.

In the sixth century, a Greek writer called Pseudo-Dionysius produced a speculative spiritual hierarchy of nine angelic orders. This is about as much use as the famous medieval question 'How many angels can dance on the head of a pin?'

11. Can a fallen angel be saved?

I once did a live interview for an American radio station on angels. This was the first question that the producer asked me – which was not quite what I was expecting or wished to be asked. The biblical answer appears to be – No! Such is the mercy and providence of God that all things are possible – but it seems highly unlikely.

Evil spirits are presumably fallen angels. Satan cannot

create anything. Evil Spirits must be part of the original creation – angels who fell. During deliverance sessions, evil spirits, if they actually speak, are usually terrified. In Mark 5:12 they asked to be sent into a herd of pigs; in a recent pastoral session they threatened to enter a pet rabbit. I think that all we are entitled to do when praying is to send such entities to Jesus for whatever purpose he may have for them – but I doubt that it includes salvation!

12. Why do there seem to be more angelic experiences today than for a very long time?

Many different explanations are currently on offer. People involved in the New Age movement tell us that angels are appearing to give humankind a last chance to love one another before they destroy the world through pollution and war. The Age of Aquarius is the world's last chance to sort itself out. They certainly have a point. New Age people *rightly tell us to treat the environment with much greater care.*

The problem is that even the most cursory reading of their literature, which is, of course, very varied, tells us of angels, often called Gabriel and Michael, instructing people to do things that are completely contrary to Scripture. Most of their angels, or spirit guides, are summoned to serve the purposes of those seeking help, whereas in Scripture angels are always messengers *sent* by God.

From a very different perspective, many will doubt the reality of such experiences. Neither angels nor demons fit a rational world-view, and such experiences will be discredited as naïve, medieval, or simply unbelievable. The apparent increase in such experiences can be explained as a curiously post-modern phenomenon whereby an increasingly confused and desperate world clutches at supernatural straws to try and convince itself that there might, after all, be a meaning or purpose to life.

For those for whom the teaching and authority of Scripture is normative, there is a natural desire to accept and believe in the existence of angels, and their place in the divine order and purpose of the universe and of our world. Some will be very cautious, citing Paul's warning about false miracles, signs and wonders (see 2 Thessalonians 2:9–11), and Jesus' clear teaching that near the end 'false Christs and false prophets will appear and perform great signs and miracles to deceive even the elect – if that were possible' (Matthew 24:24).

Others will be wildly optimistic, seeing evidence of increased angelic authority as a sign of the nearness of the return of Jesus. They will cite Jesus' words, '… learn this lesson from the fig tree: As soon as its twigs get tender and its leaves come out, you will know that summer is near. Even so, when you see all these things, you know that it is near, right at the door' (Matthew 24:32–33).

Another, rather simpler, explanation, is that we are living in an age which is *far less rational and more open to these sorts of experiences*, consequently far more people experience them, and are prepared to talk about them. Also, in the age of the Internet, people readily exchange information about angels. What, in days of the past, would have been very private experiences, now are often in the public domain. It could also be said that books like this one are adding to the exchange of information, and helping some people to be far more open to this aspect of divine communication.

My own view inclines strongly towards this last explanation. I remain very sceptical about any angelic messages purporting to tell us that the second coming is imminent.

Such teaching is contrary to Scripture (see earlier, page 170).

13. Does it matter what we believe about angels? Shouldn't we be getting on with more important matters?

There are huge issues facing our planet. As I write, another G8 summit is taking place where massive issues such as global warming, 'Make Poverty History' and Third World debt will be discussed. While there is some goodwill between the leaders of the powerful nations and many good intentions to solve the world's problems, many of the underlying issues are spiritual. Justice, climate change, looking after the planet, improving the situation for the poorer nations, are all deeply theological and moral issues.

The Bible teaches us about a God who has revealed himself supernaturally, but who also expects his people to act with justice and compassion. Belief in the existence of angels is an important part of biblical revelation. If we believe in angels, we are more likely to believe in the miracles of Jesus and his resurrection. If we believe in the resurrection, then we will believe that our life has both a purpose and a destiny. If we believe this, we are more likely to work effectively for the good of humankind.

There are, as always, two equal and opposite errors that we can fall into. On the one hand, we may be so caught up with supercharged spiritual events – such as visions, dreams and supernatural encounters – that we never get involved in the real problems of the world. Alternatively, we may be so busy trying to solve the world's problems in our own strength that we do little more than pay lip service to the Creator.

A thought-out belief in angels should help give us both hope and inspiration for daily living at both a personal and global level. For instance on page 32 I cited an example where two people, independently, saw an angel with Jackie Pullinger as she was speaking at a conference. Jackie is internationally renowned for her work amongst the drug addicts of the walled city in Hong Kong. She is able, under God, to do this work precisely because she believes in the supernatural power of prayer to help deal with addiction. Belief in angels, in particular, and the supernatural, in general, tend to inspire people to effective action.

14. I haven't seen an angel – does it mean that I am an inferior Christian?

I hope not! Writing as one who has not seen an angel, I take comfort from the words of Jesus to Thomas: 'Because you have seen me, you have believed; blessed are those who have not seen and yet have believed' (John 20:29). Thomas had missed out on Jesus' first resurrection appearance to the disciples but was granted a second opportunity a week later.

Angelic visitations are a sovereign act of God granted to people in a variety of situations but they are not the signs of special spiritual favour. Jesus warned his followers not to rely on doing spectacular things. He was looking for fruitful lives not dramatic wonder-workers. At the end of his famous Sermon on the Mount, Jesus said:

Not everyone who says to me, 'Lord, Lord,' will enter the kingdom of heaven, but only he who does the will of my Father who is in heaven. Many will say to me on that day, 'Lord, Lord, did we not prophesy in your name, and in your name drive out demons and perform many miracles? Then I will tell them plainly, 'I never knew you. Away from me, you evildoers!' (Matthew 7:21–23)

Paul also discouraged his hearers from seeking out strange experiences:

> Do not let anyone who delights in false humility and the worship of angels disqualify you for the prize. Such a person goes into great detail about what he has seen, and his unspiritual mind puffs him up with idle notions. He has lost connection with the Head, from whom the whole body, supported and held together by its ligaments and sinews, grows as God causes it to grow. (Colossians 2:18–19)

I have been impressed with the testimonies, and more importantly, the lives of those who have shared with me their angelic encounters. They have been very fortunate that God has blessed and protected them in this way. I have been equally impressed with many who have followed Jesus faithfully through dark and difficult times without any supernatural signs.

God knows us intimately (see Psalm 139) and he knows what is best for each of us on our journey of faith. For believers he has 'plans to prosper and not to harm' (Jeremiah 29:11). This is not a guarantee of a simple life, nor of angelic protection in all circumstances; but it is a guarantee that life has a purpose and that ultimately however bleak life seems 'God works for the good of those who love him, who have been called according to his purpose' (Romans 8:28).

Concluding Thoughts

Truth, reality, fruit and significance

HAVING PRESENTED MANY STORIES (and space has prevented the use of many others), I want to ask four questions. Are these accounts true? Were they the result of chance coincidence or spiritual reality? What was the outcome of these encounters in the lives of the people who were involved? What is the significance of these stories?

Truth
I believe that the witnesses are people of integrity. To take just three – Courtney, the little girl (page 83), who was travelling in a vehicle which fell off a bridge in Papua New Guinea is hardly likely to emerge from a terrifying encounter inventing a story about seeing angels. In a state of shock, immediately after the rescue, she is a reliable witness to a surprising event. We should take the witness of children very seriously in these matters and remember the words of Jesus in Matthew 18:10.

Mark (page 30), an intellectual student who was having uncertainties about his faith, is not going to base his life and calling to Christian ministry on a false account of a late-night angelic visitation. His account offers no middle way – it is either true or false. There is no possibility of delusion or mistaken identity. The encounter was unexpected, decisive and dramatic.

Ian McCormack (page 138) is not going to tramp the world telling a false account of events in Mauritius in 1982.

To me, the most remarkable part of the whole story is not his dramatic conversion, nor his experience of the world, nor even his healing. The detail about his mother being woken up in New Zealand and being told by a voice to pray for him is breathtaking. His story, too, offers no middle way. It is either true or false.

Reality

I believe these stories record real spiritual encounters. It is difficult to believe that these three, and most of the others recorded in this book and the countless others who have shared their stories with me and other people, were mere coincidences. It is just possible to believe that the Greek lawyer (page 70) or the Nigerian boy with the black bag (page 34) turned up by chance with the right skills and the right equipment to rescue an evangelist and a member of the House of Lords. But it is impossible to believe that a woman in rural Zambia (page 15) could speak English, an unknown and unheard language, in an Oxbridge accent unless the phenomena were caused by a controlling spirit.

We are dealing with spiritual realities, albeit unusual ones. This is important because the literal truth of these stories is powerful evidence pointing to a largely unseen spiritual world. The Bible constantly bears witness to this, and peoples of most races (with the notable exception of our greedy self-centred Western culture) have always believed and still believe in such matters.

Fruit

I believe that these encounters bore fruit in people's later lives. Of course, some people have amazing spiritual encounters and later turn away from God and/or put them down to coincidence.

But to meet Brothers Yun and Xu (page 52) is to encounter two people who might have stepped out of the pages of the New Testament. To meet the late James Chungolo (page 21) is to encounter someone who radiated love and a spiritual presence which bore fruit in many other people's lives. To know Pat (page 36) is to know someone for whom angelic experiences in youth has sharpened her faith and spiritual perception in later life. The grace of God touches people in many ways. When God chooses to allow his angels to intervene, the effect in people's lives is usually very wonderful.

Significance

The Christian gospel is about revelation – God speaking to humankind, principally through the teaching, the life, the death and the resurrection of Jesus Christ. Angels are a significant part of this revelation. Although their main role is worship in the courts of heaven, they are also on duty on earth. For the most part, their service to us (see Psalm 91:11 and Psalm 34:7) is largely unseen, but from time to time they are permitted to appear to instruct, guide, warn and protect.

The Bible is also clear about the dark side of angelic activity. Mark's Gospel, for instance, is a profound account of the conflict between the kingdom of God and the kingdom of Satan. I hope that the accounts in this book may both encourage faith in Jesus and warn about the dangers of stepping outside God's boundaries. The encouraging stories of the first seven chapters must be balanced with the sober warnings of the next two.

Angelic encounters today should encourage us to take the far more important angelic encounters of the Bible seriously. The angels in the shepherd's field outside Bethlehem and the angels beside the empty tomb in Jerusalem, in about AD 30, point to an eternal truth. *This affects the destiny of the whole of humankind.* If the angels on the pages of this book help anyone believe, and respond to the gospel, then they will have served a double purpose.

Those who have seen angels are in a minority; but that is no reason to doubt their testimony. Angelic encounters are never an end in themselves; but they can and should be spurs to greater spiritual commitment.

In the mathematical theory of Chaos, it is said that a butterfly flapping its wings in South America can trigger a hurricane in Africa. The tiniest actions can have dramatic consequences. In the post-modern world of today, if someone sees or senses an angel, winged or not, they will probably be inspired to attempt something beautiful for God. True spiritual encounters, whether angelic or otherwise, should have profound consequences.

THINKING CLEARLY ABOUT ANGELS

John Woolmer

If you have enjoyed Angels of Glory and Darkness, you may also wish to read John Woolmer's more extensive treatment on the same subject. A good deal of the narrative illustration is common to both books, but Thinking Clearly about Angels also provides additional biblical and theological material.

"An intelligent book by a gifted writer with a healthy streak of cynicism. You will not be able to put it down." - *Canon Michael Green, Senior Research Fellow, Wycliffe Hall, Oxford*

"Unputdownable ... no one who reads this book will ever forget it." - *Bishop David Pytches*

In the Bible, angels are seen as messengers of the Lord, executors of God's judgement, and worshippers in the courts of heaven. They can protect and guide the human race. Jesus mentions angels a number of times. Angels are a natural part of his theological understanding and experience.

Not all angels are benign, however. Some rebelled against God, and may go disguised: Paul warns, "Satan himself masquerades as an angel of light."

From extensive research, personal stories, and careful consideration of biblical sources, John Woolmer has compiled this study of the interaction of angels and humankind. "In Scripture, and I believe in present-day experience, angels come unexpectedly both to stir people into action, and to bring a much-needed sense of awe and reverence into daily living."

"Unusual, gripping and stimulating... reading this book will strengthen your faith that God is actively at work in this world." - *John Hosier, New Frontiers International*

Published by Monarch Books

ISBN-13: 978 1 85424 606 6
ISBN-10: 1 85424 606 2